BLOODY BR

HISTORY

STAFFORD

BLOODY BRITISH HISTORY
HISTORY

STAFFORD

ANTHONY POULTON-SMITH

The History Press

First published in 2013

The History Press
The Mill, Brimscombe Port
Stroud, Gloucestershire, GL5 2QG
www.thehistorypress.co.uk

British Library Cataloguing in Publication Data.
A catalogue record for this book is available from the British Library.

ISBN 978 0 7524 9083 0

Typesetting and origination by The History Press
Printed in Great Britain

CONTENTS

99 BC

IRON AGE STAFFORD

THE PROBLEM WITH telling the story of Iron Age Stafford is the lack of a permanent settlement. As the name given to the era tells us, this was a time when bronze was no longer the only metal produced by smelting – now the much stronger iron was available. The changes in everyday life could be compared to the advancements in the twentieth century, which saw steam and gas lighting become virtually obsolete as electrical power was harnessed.

That there is no evidence of Celtic culture in the county, save for the Romano-British settlements of *Letocetum* near Lichfield in the south and in the north Rocester and Chesterton, is down to the lack of local materials for the production of iron during this period.

The local Celtic tribe were the Cornovii, their territory extending over Cheshire, Shropshire and across what is now the border into Wales. While they had no coinage they were certainly wealthy enough. Fundamentally an agrarian economy, they were renowned cattle breeders, and also produced vast amounts of salt from their lands in Cheshire. Records from the Greeks and Romans show they had a network of paved roads along which they distributed the salt.

The idea these were naked, painted savages is completely wrong. Read Roman writings and it is obvious that they considered the natives 'vain' and much concerned with appearance and personal hygiene. The Cornovii excelled in weaving and dyed their cloth in the brightest of colours. Women had long hair, plaited in two lengths which often almost reached their knees. Their tribal name is thought to describe 'the people of the horned one', a reference to the

---

Stafford is an Old English place name – there was no history of 'Stafford' in 99 BC. The name did not exist until AD 913, when the first written record of *Staefford* is found.

7

image of their chief god. Although similarly-named tribes have been located in Caithness and Cornwall, there was no actual connection between the three tribes, which were as far removed as it is possible for three groups to be on the British mainland.

Little archaeological evidence has been discovered prior to the Roman occupation. For some time this was thought to indicate a lack of possessions and thus a lack of wealth. However, throughout recorded history Staffordshire has been a county with low population density. The population was further reduced by Conquest: at the time of the Domesday Survey the valuation of the parishes clearly reflect the brutal suppression of William the Conqueror.

Perhaps a lack of surviving evidence from the Celtic era is not so much because it was a period of constant conflict but quite the reverse. Indeed the few archaeological records found in the Stafford area are a result of battles. Skeletal remains showing injuries sustained in battle have been unearthed, their identity shown by the clothing and artefacts found alongside.

Most conflicts between rival tribes were ritualised. Champions and leaders fought duels after boasting of the personal achievements of their ancestors. It was the failure of these rituals which led to a full-blooded battle, and it is the remains of such we find in Stafford.

Before any actual fighting broke out the Celts would sound war horns, ride around in their chariots, and clatter weapons against wooden shields to add to the din. As the cacophony peaked, and with adrenalin flowing freely, the combatants charged and, shortly before clashing hand to hand, launched a light javelin at the foe. This tactic was primarily to distract and slow the charge rather than maim the enemy. It was in personal combat these warriors tested their prowess.

The principal weapon was the battle-axe. Doubtless the more experienced warrior had his own particular tricks of the trade but, in general terms, the winner was inevitably the one who bludgeoned his opponent first and/or hardest. Wooden shields would not offer much in the way of protection and were only really of use in deflecting the blow. A short handle made it easier to wield, especially in tight quarters.

Examining the skeletons shows most blows were delivered with a downward movement and principally to the area of the neck and ribcage. Other axe marks are found to the arms and legs: these were designed to impair movement and produce an advantage rather than to kill. A successful hit at the neck or shoulder would cleave the opponent in two, with death inevitable – and hopefully mercifully quick. We also find evidence of ribs broken by feet as the victor braced himself against his victim in order to retrieve the blade buried so deeply into the torso.

During this period the spiritual side of life was, sources lead us to believe, primarily influenced by the druids, though virtually nothing is known of their rites and practices at the time. Virtually everything attributed to this period was written by the Romans much later: contemporary Greek reports speak of druids as priests who dabbled in rites more associated with magic but admit little is definitely known about them.

These Celtic peoples could never have been a part of the Roman Empire, for the first Roman emperor was not in power until 27 BC. From the founding of Rome in 753 BC until 509 BC Rome was a kingdom. In between, which includes 99 BC, it was the Roman Republic.

Named Celtic deities are generally those worshipped by the Gauls in France, most of which were also common to the pagan Roman religion. It was when the Romans came to Britannia that the druids were hunted down and eventually forced to retreat to the island of Anglesey off the north coast of Wales. Legends of their defence, and the horrific slaughter which ensued, are predominantly based on the reports of Tacitus, the authenticity of which is questionable.

AD 99

ROMAN STAFFORD

BEGINNING IN THE eighth century BC, the Roman Empire had spread to encompass much of the known western world by AD 43. While Julius Caesar had planned to cross the English Channel almost a century earlier, his fleeting attempts were scuppered as much by his misunderstanding of the tides as the fierce defiance of the native Britons.

This may sound odd but until the Romans moved away from the Mediterranean they never experienced the twice-daily movement of the tides, for the Mediterranean has none. Envisage beaching your vessel and letting the troops embark at low tide. Returning six hours later, you would find the tide at full height. With no anchor used to secure it, your boat would have floated away or been crushed against the land.

Before looking at the Romans in Stafford, we should also mention AD 16. In this year there is a record of the ships commanded by Tiberius. While engaged in campaigns in what is now modern Germany, the fleet was swept westwards by a sudden storm and was washed up on the shores of Britain. However, the brave Roman legionnaires did not sweep all before them in a heroic march across Britannia. Having met the rulers of local tribes, they returned meekly to Europe telling tales of a land dominated by hideous monsters.

Twenty-seven years later they arrived and were to stay for a little under four centuries. While there is no question that a number of tribes were fervently opposed to the 'invasion', at least as many welcomed the opportunity for trade as part of a vast empire. Joining the European Common Market in 1973

Tiberius Avidius Quietus was the Roman Governor in charge of Britain in AD 99. He was uncle to Emperor Hadrian's daughter-in-law, and was well acquainted with the Greek historian Plutarch and the Roman Senator Pliny the Younger.

In AD 99 the year was not recorded as AD 99, but as 'the Year of the Consulship of Palma and Senecio' or sometimes 'Year 852 *Ab urbe condita*' meaning 'from the founding of the City of Rome'.

Roman soldiers. (Courtesy of the Thomas Fisher Rare Book Library, University of Toronto)

was a drop in the ocean compared with uniting with the Roman Empire 1,563 years earlier!

Just how many troops arrived, or even where they landed, is unrecorded. Indeed, all we are certain of is that a single legion was here. This was the II Augusta commanded by Vespasian, who was to become emperor twenty-six years later. Aulus Plautinus was in charge of the invasion itself and probably dripped a supply of soldiers across the Channel rather than send a mass attack.

Perhaps the stories from Tiberius' troops had reached their ears, especially as we know that the troops mutinied shortly before their intended departure.

It is impossible to know when what is now Stafford saw its first Roman, or even when the first settlement was created here. However, as Boudica and the Iceni were defeated at Mancetter near Atherstone in AD 60 or 61, it is safe to assume that they had reached Stafford before then. They had probably constructed a settlement or camp, be it temporary or permanent, by

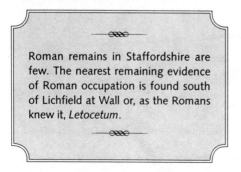

Roman remains in Staffordshire are few. The nearest remaining evidence of Roman occupation is found south of Lichfield at Wall or, as the Romans knew it, *Letocetum*.

this time. It seems unlikely the archaeological evidence dates from the early occupations: the following details will therefore be from a later time at the end of the first century.

Excavations at Clark Street revealed evidence of occupation during the Roman era. Archaeologists discovered a layer containing Saxon remains; the dominant features were four post holes indicating a permanent structure. These holes had been driven through what had previously been sealed by weathering, the passage of time and post-Roman cultivation.

In 1985 archaeologists removed the fill from the post holes, took soil samples from the sides of these holes and sent these for radiocarbon dating. These revealed a date of the late first century AD. Subsequently these earlier levels were excavated and Romano-British pottery remains discovered. Under a microscope organic material was found, including fragments of charcoal and grains.

Another building was found in St Mary's Grove. Here post holes contained Saxon remains and, once again, Romano-British pottery was discovered below the cap created by much later farming activity. A larger piece of Roman pottery dating from the second century was discovered near St Mary's church, with a third-century coin uncovered a little further away. In another dig near the former Stafford Gaol, at what once was the Hanging Ditch public house, archaeologists discovered a tessellated pavement, a conclusive sign of long-term Roman occupation.

In AD 410, with Rome in trouble, the outpost of Britannia was abandoned. While the military presence had gone, the Romano-British culture endured. Moreover, although it is often imagined that the Saxons invaded as soon as the proverbial Roman back was turned, in truth the Saxon culture took a long time to become dominant.

Eventually the Roman roads became overgrown and the houses and other structures fell into disrepair and/or were disassembled for rebuilding. Although it did not happen overnight, the simple truth is the Romano-British way of life ended because those remaining on our island simply forgot the skills required to be Roman.

AD 913

LADY OF THE MERCIANS

IN AD 913, Stafford was ruled by a warrior queen: Aethelfled, the 'Lady of the Mercians'. By the time we find the first mention of Aethelfled, roughly the year 890, she was already married. Her husband Aethelred was by then Ealdorman of Mercia, and they were living in the palaces of the Saxon kingdom of Mercia with their daughter Aelfwynn.

Although her date of birth is not recorded, we know she was the first child of Ealhswith and Alfred. This was none other than King Alfred, the only English monarch ever styled 'the Great', and the man who did more to unify England than any other. Her brother, Edward the Elder, succeeded his father as king of Wessex and of the English. His eldest son, Aethelstan, followed after Edward, although Aethelfled had virtually raised her nephew in their Mercian court.

Alfred had sought an agreement with the invading Vikings. War was expensive and a negotiated settlement also saved lives. The eventual peace agreement was based around the Danes agreeing to convert to Christianity, a stipulation which, in itself, helped to retain the peace.

With Alfred's death came unrest and Edward the Elder had to contend with renewed problems from the Danes. Aethelred died in Mercia in 911, leaving Aethelfled to rule as Lady of the Mercians. This was no courtesy title: she had a well-deserved reputation as an accomplished tactician and military leader and, during the next eight years of her time at the helm, she built a

Statue of Aethelfled outside the castle at Tamworth.

This piece of wood, discovered during the dig for Bertilin's chapel, may look old, but it is simply a representation of the much earlier cross lying several feet below.

series of fortresses to defend the region of Mercia against threat. Chroniclers speak of the construction of Bridgnorth, Tamworth, Eddisbury, Warwick, Chirbury, and Runcorn fortresses, and three others, thus far undiscovered, which were erected at Bremesburh, Scergeat and Weardbyrig.

Another fort was built at what is now known as Stafford. In 913 Aethelfled had already chosen the easiest site to defend, realising that a natural sandbank, formed in a bend of the River Sow and surrounding marshland, would provide an ideal location. Prior to this, Stafford had been a very lonely place indeed,

home to a small religious community. To suddenly find themselves amidst a section of the Mercian army must have come as a huge culture shock, although they may eventually have come to recognise that it made them much safer.

The original town was constructed between two points: the northern part of Greengate Street and Bridge Street shortly before it reaches the Sow. The southern and western borders were covered by the Sow and by marshland which, combined with the construction of a defensive barrier around the whole settlement, made the residents much safer from attack. Indeed, when word went out that the area was under threat, the new Stafford offered a comparatively safe haven for surrounding villages and hamlets.

The Lady of the Mercians also built a church. It was dedicated to St Bertilin, an early English saint already linked to the area. This may have been a new settlement, and Church records indicate no less than thirteen priests were housed here. Furthermore, a mint was striking coinage here soon afterwards, a clear indication of wealth and success.

Together with similar fortresses in neighbouring Cheshire and Shropshire, this chain of fortresses proved a notable deterrent to the Danes. This plan was hatched entirely by Aethelfled. She not only worked out where the fortresses should be located from a strategic standpoint, but envisaged and designed the whole line in her head with information gleaned solely from what she had seen on her travels.

On 12 June 918, with Aethelfled's influence giving Saxons everywhere renewed hope of defeating the Danes,

The present church on this site is dedicated to St Mary.

The outline of St Bertilin's chapel in the grounds of the present-day St Mary's church, as discovered on the archaeological dig of 1954.

the Lady of the Mercians died at Tamworth. She was buried at what was then St Peter's church and is now St Oswald's Priory in Gloucester. Her final resting place is a fitting tribute to this remarkable woman. What had been a Roman city was rebuilt under the watchful eye of Aethelfled, adhering closely to the earlier street plan and still very clear today.

Just a month after Aethelfled's death, Pope Anastasius III died and was succeeded by the 121st holder of this office, Pope Lando. The latter was only to be pope for seven months but still managed to leave his mark. Firstly he was one of the few popes to use his own name. Furthermore, until the election of John Paul in 1978, he was the last pope not to require a number; he was the first pope of this name. If any reader is thinking of becoming the first Pope Archie or even Pope Annette, perhaps they should consider the short terms of the previous 'firsts'. Pope Lando's seven months seems an eternity when compared with the fleeting thirty-three days of Pope John Paul, hardly time to get the seat warm.

AD 1069

THE BATTLE OF STAFFORD

GENERALLY SPEAKING, THE Normans were not resoundingly welcomed to our shores. Yet it is also true to say that the lives of the majority in England hardly changed at all. Most people worked the land, managing to eke out a living simply by growing enough to support their family and pay a proportion to the lord of the manor. As far as the political situation was concerned, they had no time and likely no interest in who sat on the throne.

Yet this was not true of the tribal leaders. Many rebelled against the new regime, including, most famously, Hereward the Wake around the Isle of Ely whose stubborn resistance has been told many times. Further west another ,less well-known battle was fought, albeit with the same eventual results, when rebel forces gathered from Staffordshire, Herefordshire and Shropshire and, supported by a large quota from over the Welsh border, rose up under the leadership of Edric the Wild.

Little is known of Edric before his uprising. He certainly was not at Hastings and there is some evidence to suggest he had held the position of the Bishop of Worcester's 'shipman'. If this was the case he would have been at sea when the Saxon and Norman forces were battling on 14 October 1066. However, the following year his holdings were affected when two Norman earls annexed his lands. Edric's reaction to this event was to be so violent that he earned the name by which he is remembered – 'the Wild'.

With the sons of the late King Harold returning from battling in the West

---

Edric the Wild certainly existed, although a fair amount of his apparent exploits appear in writing for the first time in the thirteenth century. This has led to speculation that Edric was being credited with events which should have been attributed to others. Others have gone further and suggested these rebellious tales were the beginnings of the legend of the most famous outlaw of Norman England, the legendary Robin Hood.

Country, and with King William busy fighting the earls of Northumbria and Mercia, Edric and his Welsh allies came northeast from their strongholds in the Marcher lands. First they took Shrewsbury, and later Chester. William, leaving much of his army to the east, personally brought a force across the Pennines to face Edric and his allies.

Nobody really knows where the Battle of Stafford was fought. Nor is there any record of the numbers that took part, but it must have been a substantial figure as the armies of the two principal combatants were supported by Earl Brian riding up from the West Country, in the case of King William, and Saxons of Cheshire and Staffordshire behind Edric the Wild. After a bloody meeting, the latter retreated with his Welsh allies to the hills, leaving his men to be slaughtered. Accepting the inevitability of defeat by the Normans, Edric not only gave up the fight but even joined the king on his brief excursion into Scotland.

All this conflict by and against Norman rule would be quelled inside a year. Over the winter of 1069-70 William and his troops embarked on a campaign against the former kingdoms of the north. Known as the 'Harrowing of the North', it is estimated some 100,000 people died during these few short months. Yet it is impossible to quantify the numbers that suffered in and around Stafford because of the scorched earth policy.

While details of the Battle of Stafford are sketchy, the repercussions are very clear. Even fifteen years later the Domesday survey records Staffordshire as having fewer entries than any county except Middlesex and Rutland, which

William the Conqueror. (THP)

are much smaller. More than a half of the settlements listed were valued at under £2, a paltry sum even in 1086. Furthermore, one-fifth of this larger-than-average county was described as 'waste', with Stafford remaining by far the largest settlement and yet with a population of 1,000 maximum.

The scenes of devastation across most of the county must have been appalling and we can only guess at the horrors witnessed at the Battle of Stafford. Vegetation recovers quite quickly and yet, by the time of the Domesday Book, much of the county was not only more suited to native deer, wild boar, and packs of wolves than to people, but also most certainly overwhelmed by them. Estimates of the degree of devastation vary, but it was a minimum of two centuries before the area had recovered

William the Conqueror died in September 1086. His grave has hardly been treated with respect: the pope ordered it to be opened in 1522; then, forty years later, it was opened again during the French Wars of Religion when the remains were scattered. As a result, the only known remains are a thigh bone (which showed the king to have been quite tall and robust for his time, standing at least 5ft 10in tall). This would tend to support the story of his burial, which tells how his remains had to be crammed into his coffin as it was too small. This resulted in the now swollen body bursting, spreading a most awful smell throughout the church.

sufficiently to bring the quality of life back to the level enjoyed before the arrival of the Normans.

It was almost inevitable Edric would become a part of folklore. Some speak of his marriage to a fairy or elfin maiden. Gondul, as she is known, is said to ride alongside him into battle. This is not only an ancient legend. Several reports of more recent activity include those of Edric the Wild riding the battlefields in the weeks before the Crimean War, the First World War and even the Second World War.

AD 1399

THE KING HAS BEEN CAPTURED

Richard II led in chains through Stafford

THIS KING OF England came to the throne in 1377. Yet, as he was only ten years of age at the time, his reign was led by a number of specially appointed councils. Richard's uncle, John of Gaunt, remained a very important figure and, while never officially appointed regent, it cannot be denied he was just as influential.

Richard's reign was to be one of unrest: in 1397, after a failed rebellion, Richard executed or exiled many of his council, the 'Lords Appellant'. Then he cut off the inheritance of his cousin,

Henry Bolinbroke. This resulted in Henry leading an invasion of England in June 1399, purporting to be an attempt to reclaim his birthright but actually the first in a series of events culminating in Richard being deposed and Henry IV taking the ultimate prize of the throne.

When Henry arrived in England he found varying degrees of support from disgruntled nobles who swelled his initially small force. Richard was met by Henry at Flint Castle where – or so it was later claimed – he offered his abdication if Henry would spare his life.

John of Gaunt died in this year. This was significant, as he had been the most powerful figure in the land during the fourteenth century. His family not only numbered those who ruled England but, through an illegitimate line named Beaufort, took the crown of Scotland. Eventually the two nations were united and the heraldic symbol used by John of Gaunt began to appear everywhere. It continues to be seen today as the most popular pub name in the land, the Red Lion.

John of Gaunt. (THP)

Richard II. (THP)

London. Rumblings of counter revolt and justifiable questions as to the legitimacy of Henry's right to the throne forced his hand. It has been suggested that Richard again offered to abdicate on 29 September, the day before the new king was officially recognised by Parliament and exactly a fortnight

Richard was marched, under guard, to London – and the route took them through Stafford. While later reports suggested he rode immediately behind the future Henry IV, these are less reliable than local and contemporary records which tell of the king being brought through the streets as a prisoner. Stripped of the trappings associated with this rank of the nobility, the former monarch was trussed up and paraded through the streets. His captors milked the audience to the maximum. Whilst their progress was naturally slowed by the narrow streets, the procession's progress was quite obviously unnatural. Clearly the intention was to humiliate the fallen king.

Richard arrived in London on 1 September that year and was immediately imprisoned in the Tower of

The most powerful man in England in the fourteenth century: John of Gaunt's memorial. (Courtesy of the Thomas Fisher Rare Book Library, University of Toronto)

Isabella of Valois was the second wife of Richard II, having married him when she was just six years of age; she was widowed at the age of nine. Her younger sister, Catherine of Valois, also became queen consort when she married Henry V, the eldest son of Henry IV.

before his coronation. The deposed king was moved to Pontefract Castle at the end of the year. Just what happened in the interim ten weeks is as unknown as the journey and the details of his incarceration. Perhaps there is some truth in the idea he was simply locked away and eventually starved to death. Without anyone tending to his needs, and with no one guarding his prison, the chances of Richard's location being given away by those employed to keep him secure were few.

King Richard II is thought to have breathed his last on 14 February 1400. His corpse was eventually taken to Kings Langley church, where he was buried in early March. Sadly nobody recorded the thoughts of the people of Stafford who saw him paraded through the streets of the town six months earlier. Which Richard did they see? Was he the proud

> Wiliam le Scrope, 1st Duke of Wiltshire, was also executed this year. Captured in Bristol Castle, he and two fellow close associates of Richard II, Sir John Bussy and Sir Henry Green, were executed without trial. Their heads were taken to London and displayed on London Bridge. Six months after their execution all three were found guilty by parliament and their estates forfeited to the Crown.

aristocrat, defiant to the last (despite his predicament)? Or was this a broken and frightened man wishing for a quick end to his inevitable suffering? Either way, the next six months must have been a terrible torment for this usurped King of England.

AD 1560

CAPITAL OF FILTH!

The Horrors of Stafford's Unsanitary Streets

WHAT WOULD TODAY be considered bye-laws were once enforced with the utmost severity – such oddities as washing tripe in the local stream or river (good for the tripe washer, but not so good for those downstream who relied on this as a source of clean water).

Whilst we would never associate the sixteenth century with high standards of sanitation, there were rules and regulations in place to maintain the standards set. What is more, they were very keen to ensure these were obeyed. In much the same way as litter bugs face prosecution today, law enforcement officers of yesteryear threw the proverbial book at those failing to follow sanitation laws. Thankfully a record of proceedings from 1560 has survived to the present day.

This record concerns one sitting of the Court Baron of Stafford, the findings and the judgements passed. Not only does the record speak of those brought to task but also the remedies taken to ensure problems were resolved. Clearly no minutes were maintained: only the problems and the resulting findings are known. However, it does enable us to produce a virtual newspaper article reporting on the events on this particular day some four and half centuries later.

Stafford was a town surrounded by a wall. This was nothing unusual: most towns had a wall around them, though not as a military feature – these were there to protect the town's economy, and anyone passing in or out had to pay the required tolls and levies. However, the temptation to dump rubbish outside

---

Pirates began to make their influence felt in the Caribbean this year. These were fundamentally a collection of shipwrecked English, French and Dutch sailors (including some from Staffordshire), whose name, 'buccaneers', came from the French *boucan*, a wooden frame set over a fire on which meat was smoked. Those who smoked the meat were known as *boucaniers*, which became 'buccaneers'.

Part of the old town wall.

the wall, where it became someone else's problem, proved too much for some. This problem was particularly severe at Cooke's Walls, where a Mr Bayleys was charged with ensuring this was eradicated.

A more common problem in the days before adequate sewers was the sewage in the town. For years all waste had been thrown into the street. While rainwater and traffic would wash some things from the surface, it was by no means sufficient. Hence the court decreed that the emptying of privies and tubs (toilets and sinks) in the streets would incur a fine. Privies were not the only place where people relieved themselves. The Tudors were keen to set standards and went to great lengths to ensure it was no longer considered good etiquette to allow one corner of the room to double

as an impromptu urinal. Not only was it in bad taste but it would undoubtedly lead to the rotting of the floorboards – with disastrous consequences. They went on to state, having prevented the slow destruction of wooden floors, that 'pyssynge in chymnes' (chimneys) was equally distasteful.

The court took pains to point out the 'mastife dogg suffered to goo abroode in the nyght tyme' was not to be tolerated. It is clear the actual problem was dogs allowed to run free at night. The mastiff was a very popular breed at the time, but the rule was not restricted to mastiffs alone.

One Mr Baylif Dorryngtone was forbidden from keeping any more pigsties against the property of one John Fox. Failure to comply would result in the forfeiting of said property

> Amy Robsart died this year. This English noblewoman was the wife of the Lord Robert Dudley, a favourite of Queen Elizabeth I. Amy did not follow her husband to court, where he was to be made Master of the Horse, as she was said to be suffering from a mystery illness. Courtiers were convinced the Queen, already known to be in love with Dudley, would marry him when his wife's death was announced. When Amy did not die from this mystery illness but from an even more suspicious fall – down a staircase, resulting in a broken neck – the rumour mill soon suggested she had been murdered…

to the court. The same would befall the Chamberlayne family should they not provide a bridge across the water in Cotton Field. It was also decreed that they should make a pair of butts, to prevent the sewage from spreading, before Pentecost.

The courts were not only anxious to stop any further build-up of rubbish but to clear that already accumulated. John Perker was paid ten shillings to construct a ditch on both sides of his garden, channels to act as simple sewers. Richard Wayt received tuppence to clear the muck from his barn. One Thomas Watwood was paid two shillings to 'washe clean Salter Street'. A Thomas Waltho was paid three shillings and fourpence to move his pig sty 2ft further away before next Pentecost. (It would be a simple task to work out the date of Pentecost, but not to explain just what the sty had to be moved 2ft further away from…)

Neighbours Henry Savage, Robert Hartell and all others having their houses, stables, gardens, etc., in the same street were ordered to clean up said street. They were also to keep it so or would face a fine of twelve pence each. Others were ordered to ensure problems did not arise in either Bere Lane or the churchyard.

The court's resolve was clear. Raw sewage in the streets and dumped outside the town walls was unacceptable, completely unsanitary, and had to be sorted out as soon as possible.

AD 1625

CESS AND THE CITY!

The Most Bizarre Map in Stafford's History Revealed

'**T**HE ONLY TWO** certainties in life are death and taxes' is a statement often attributed to Mark Twain. However, he had not even been born when it first appeared, in a letter written by Benjamin Franklin to Jean-Baptiste Leroy – a prominent French scientist of the time. A particularly gloomy outlook and one which fails to take the human digestive system into consideration.

On average, an adult human produces some 2,500 gallons of urine per annum. Each individual also manages to contribute almost 200-weight of solid waste to the mix. This has to go somewhere – and a map of Stafford in 1625 went to great lengths to show exactly where. In towns the majority of this human waste was collected in cesspits. Theoretically this was collected and disposed of away from the town. In practice, it was left until it became an unbearable nuisance, having overflowed.

The Stafford map of 1625 shows a channel in the middle of the main High Street through the town. Certainly this was cut for drainage but it would also have contained rubbish of all description,

both vegetable and animal matter, manure from livestock and horses, and undoubtedly human waste. Residents must have both longed for and dreaded rain: too little and the channel would never be cleared; too much and the channel would overflow. This is Britain: it never rains just the right amount!

We know there was one cesspit beneath what is now Marks & Spencer's: it was found during the building of the famous store in 1932. It was a square

The Ancient High House would not have been known as such: it was a very new building in 1625.

THE EVENTS OF THE YEAR

Charles I succeeded to the throne on 27 March, following the death of his father James I of England and VI of Scotland. His accession to the throne was much quieter than the Civil War and regicide which brought an end to his reign.

Meanwhile, William Oughtred, English mathematician, invented the slide rule this year. Obsolete since the invention of the calculator, it was once the alternative to the book of logarithms, tangents, sines and cosines, and only ever used by the kid who wanted to show off.

pit, lined with bricks, so some seepage into the surrounding earth was inevitable. When it overflowed the ordure would likely have found its way to the channel, or at least eventually.

Those employed to empty the cesspits were known as gongfermors. They, as with the night-soil men who were to follow, chiefly worked at night. This reduced the problem of smell and helped avoid the nuisance of flies.

The map shows the channel draining away to the south. Indeed, it runs through the town wall at Southgate almost directly opposite the bridge over the River Sow. Of course the channel emptied into the river, taking anything the flow was strong enough to carry with it. Pollution was a very real problem, not

The River Sow.

only at this point but further upstream as the water was undrinkable. Even animals refused to touch it. We know this because the map of 1625 points out that men crossed the bridge over the River Sow every day to take their horses to drink.

The High Street channel, along with a number of others, all drained into the river, but this was not the only problem. As already noted, the cesspits were also emptied, albeit irregularly. The contents were removed outside the walls of the town to the communal dung heap. This was located just downstream of the bridge at Southgate and identified on the map.

This same feature is also described as 'the way to the Thieves' Ditch'. The name is not fully understood, having at least two possible meanings. Possibly this tells of a route used by thieves to enter the town by which there was much less chance of being seen. The second, more gruesome, explanation makes far more sense. With so many crimes incurring the death penalty, and the criminals denied a burial in consecrated ground, it may be that this was an area set aside for the foulest and most odious of human rubbish – corpses.

AD 1643

SIEGE OF STAFFORD CASTLE

VISUALLY, STAFFORD'S CASTLE appears to be the quintessential stone-built fortress. Sitting atop the castle mound, it appears as solid and impregnable as ever. On one side this vantage point overlooks the town and Cannock Chase beyond; to the other, the expanse of the Staffordshire Moorlands. Yet things are not quite what they seem.

As a defensive feature, the records begin in the 1080s with Robert de Tosny, as a motte and bailey designed to act as a warning to troublesome locals. Little or no stone was used: this was earth and timber with large defensive ditches. It could have been added to a much earlier Celtic settlement (although no archaeological evidence has been found to substantiate this claim).

For the next two centuries there is little recorded about the castle. Then, in 1348, John of Bicester built a stone castle based on the Norman layout. His task was recorded in an agreement as 'building a castle on the mound within the manor of Stafford, in length, breadth and height, with towers, rooms, bedchambers, chapel, privies, chimneys, loopholes, windows, doors, and gates'.

It is interesting to note how bedchambers precede the chapel and privies are listed ahead of windows and doors.

Much of what stood then would be recognisable today, yet this is misleading since the present-day building dates from 1813 when owner Edward Jerningham commissioned the rebuilding of the castle in the fourteenth-century style. Hence what we see today is a folly or, more correctly, what remains after nineteenth and twentieth-century wear and tear, and the dismantling of the upper parts of the towers by the army in the 1960s.

However, it is the seventeenth century which interests us, and the castle as it was in 1643. This was a time of Civil War and

> The 4 January saw the birth of a man who remains one of the most famous scientists in world history. Sir Isaac Newton is undoubtedly best-remembered for the apple which is supposed to have fallen on his head, resulting in the discovery of gravity.

Above *Stafford Castle today. (Giles Jones)*

Right *Civil War battle in full flight: this shows Hopton Heath, a famous Staffordshire skirmish.*

in the quiet political backwater that was Staffordshire one lady stood firm against the foe. A staunch Roman Catholic and Royalist, Lady Isabel Stafford was head of the household which retreated to the family castle after the town of Stafford fell to Parliamentarians on 15 May 1643 following a brief and largely bloodless siege.

Holed up in the castle, Lady Isabel was visited by Colonel Brereton, with a few of his men, who demanded her surrender. She refused. In response, Brereton set light to some of the outhouses, homes to the poor, certain this would make her change her mind. It served only to strengthen her resolve, and her troops fired several volleys at the arsonists, injuring men and horses in the process. In response Brereton ordered all the nearby dwellings to be razed to the ground.

For the next three weeks her determination and resolve to defend her home against all odds was the key factor in keeping her household from surrendering. She was certain assistance would come and reminded her followers of this every single day. She must have been either a formidable woman or one who inspired loyalty for, with food and water running low and conditions within deteriorating rapidly, surrender must have been very tempting.

It is clear the household's loyalty to Lady Isabel went above and beyond their job description. None of those holed up in the castle were trained to fight. Neither were they particularly knowledgeable when it came to medicine – not that wounds from battle needed to be treated: it was illness and disease which were proving a problem. A few years later, with the Restoration of the Monarchy, it was reported that at the time of the siege, the Lady Isabel had virtually abandoned her role as

> Another Civil War engagement was the Battle of Lansdowne on 5 July, where the official result was recorded as a draw – or perhaps neither side could be bothered to continue, as it is quite implausible to think they shook hands and went home having run out of time. Of course, a penalty shoot-out was out of the question: with both sides being English, neither would have won!

lady of the house and 'mucked in' with her staff to prepare food and tend to the sick and needy while their enemy camped without.

The Midlands was regarded as vital to both sides. As the name implies, it separates the north from the south. Thus holding the Midlands meant preventing the enemy from unifying their forces. Lichfield was held first by the Parliamentarians and then the Royalists before Brereton and Colonel Hastings clashed once again at Stafford.

Relief finally came to the Lady Isabel and her retinue when Hastings succeeded in reaching the castle on 5 June. The gallant Royalist soldier insisted upon the lady of the house leaving her home and promised to leave a garrison there to defend it, which he did. They remained here for just three weeks, but fled when, from this position, they saw a siege canon being brought toward the town and knew their time was up.

On 22 December an order from the Parliamentarians in Stafford sounded the end for the castle as a defensive feature by ordering its demolition. Contemporary reports noted that the order had been carried out without the slightest trouble, save for the loss of a crowbar!

Following the Restoration of the Monarchy, it was revealed how the most famous son of Stafford, and probably the most famous fisherman of all time, aided the Royalists. Best known for his work *The Compleat Angler*, Izaak Walton was also a staunch Royalist supporter. At great personal risk he managed to bring one of the Crown Jewels, a gem known as Little George, to London from whence it was smuggled out of the country and to the future Charles II when he was still in exile.

In the 1940s impromptu tours were offered by the then caretakers. As visitors to the castle will soon discover, in the worst of winter conditions the slope is a challenge – to say the least. Hence around the time of the Second World War, when the then caretakers declined to show some young men around, one creative vandal bent and shaped a lead pipe into a 'Stafford Knot'.

AD 1646

PLAGUES OF CHRISTMAS PAST

WE ARE HERE to travel back to a time almost exactly two centuries before Charles Dickens first published his best known work, *A Christmas Carol*. It is true to say this story from 1646 is scarier than anything the great novelist ever committed to paper.

Ever since the thirteenth century the pall of the plague had hung over Europe. While the first reference to an epidemic of the plague comes from the Byzantine Empire in the sixth century, it was during the middle of the fourteenth century when more than a third of the population of Europe succumbed to this dreadful disease.

Spread by the bites of fleas found on small rodents, the disease is marked by gangrenous attacks on the extremities, such as the fingers, toes, lips and tip of the nose as well as by muscle cramps, chills, high temperature, seizures, skin colour changes, difficulty in breathing, vomiting blood, coughing, skin decay, delirium, and for some coma. Of course the best known features are the buboes which gave bubonic plague its name. The term Black Death appears to have been coined in the 1830s – even during

the seventeenth century it was most often referred to as 'the Great Plague' or 'the Great Pestilence'. An infection of the lymph glands and produced by the colony of bacteria, these painful swellings appear at the armpits, neck, top of the legs and in the groin.

Today treatment using broad-spectrum antibiotics proves successful in nearly all cases, providing treatment begins within twenty-four hours of the onset of symptoms. In the middle of the seventeenth century any treatments were ineffective and the disease proved fatal in over 90 per cent of cases. It is not surprising that medicine was slow in producing a cure considering how rapidly the infections spread.

The suspected causes of the plague were just as ludicrous as the cures. The Jews were often blamed, a situation not helped by them being tortured until they admitted to poisoning wells; other suspects included bad air released by earthquakes, and a particularly unfavourable alignment of Mars, Jupiter and Saturn. Many doctors fervently believed bad smells would drive out the plague from a victim. Some of the most odious cocktails ever concocted, most based on dung and urine, were prepared and placed under the noses of some very ill fellows. No surprise to find this early aromatherapy was worse than useless and probably aided the spread of the disease rather than halt it. Other optimistic cures included converting to Christianity, drinking good wine, not bathing, not eating fruit, not abusing the poor, avoiding lecherous behaviour, not being in debt and, strangest of all, simply being happy.

The disease was not rife throughout the land for four centuries but came in waves. Sometimes it decimated the entire population but, as in 1646, it affected only certain parts of the country. What became known as the Great Plague of London killed about 20 per cent of the nation's capital, estimated at least 100,000 victims.

In the same year the disease was also known to be seeking victims in Stafford. Numbers of victims in Stafford at this time were much fewer, probably under 1,000, but they still represented 20 to 25 per cent of the population. To put this into perspective, this equates to losing one individual from the standard family in the modern era of two parents plus 2.4 children. It should also be noted in seventeenth-century England the number of children would usually be higher, owing to a lack of birth control.

Bodies of the victims were transported beyond the town wall and interred in a number of pits dug specifically for the purpose. The location of these pits is uncertain and yet, taking into account that the city gates at the time were north and south of the town, it seems probable these were dug nearby to take

Plague, plague and plague again! (Courtesy of the Thomas Fisher Rare Book Library, University of Toronto)

advantage of these exits. Furthermore, the marshland and rivers to the south – remembering this was also the town's main water supply – would make this a poor choice. Hence the higher ground to the north seems the logical option.

On Christmas Day of 1646, a Friday, the House of Commons sat. They ordered a collection on the following day throughout London and Westminster. What we now know as Boxing Day was then a traditional day for fasting. It was ordered that all monies collected would be channelled into helping the distressed and infected inhabitants of the town of Stafford.

Just how much this collection helped the town is impossible to say; however, it may have been the last serious outbreak in the county town as there are no records of note, and a century later the disease was no more in Britain.

THE MAN WHO KILLED A KING

John Bradshaw and the Death of Charles I

BORN IN JULY 1602 and living until October 1659, John Bradshaw's most important role in British history came in 1649. As MP for Stafford and also a judge, in this tempestuous year he was appointed president of the parliamentary commission to try Charles I.

It may sound as if he was the leading candidate for the task, yet this was not the case. Not only was he not the first to be offered the position, others having turned it down, but many considered him quite unsuitable for the role. Indeed, the king himself refused to recognise his authority as he, along with much of the court, maintained he was quite unsuitable as hardly anyone had heard of him. Bradshaw did nothing to convince anyone of his suitability – indeed, he did not even come to court until the third session, whereupon he apologised, saying he had been out of London.

When he did arrive he was clearly concerned about the repercussions of taking on the role. In court he was flanked by several personal guards, carried a sword, and wore armour under scarlet robes. He also sported a broad-brimmed, bullet-proof beaver hat – covered with velvet and lined with steel.

The trial proper began on 20 January in Westminster Hall. Eventually the charge was read – the king having interrupted the prosecutor as he attempted to do so – claiming Charles Stuart was singularly responsible for 'waging war against this Parliament and the people therein represented'. He was indicted as

Charles I towards the end of his life. (Courtesy of the Thomas Fisher Rare Book Library, University of Toronto)

'guilty of all treasons, murders, rapines, burnings, spoils, desolations, damages and mischiefs to this nation, acted and committed in the said wars, or occasioned thereby'. When the king refused to recognise the court, thus not entering a plea, he was immediately considered guilty according to the law of the day.

Witnesses were called, although not all thirty-three gave evidence in the Painted Hall and none were cross-examined by the king. Their evidence was later read out to the court officials. Commissioners heard how Charles had committed numerous atrocities, had drawn blood on the battlefield, and how he had deliberately stirred up feelings in order to continue the wars solely in his own interest. On Saturday, 27 January Bradshaw read out the verdict: 'Guilty as a tyrant, traitor, murderer and public enemy of the Commonwealth of England.' He continued to speak for forty minutes, not allowing any final words from the now sentenced prisoner as, under English law, the prisoner was considered to be already dead as soon as sentence was passed, and thus was not allowed to speak.

Charles, however, did speak three days later. He was standing on the scaffold outside the Banqueting House at Whitehall as he told the crowd that his actions had been to ensure the freedom of his subjects, but 'their liberty and freedom consists in having government. It is not their having a share in the government; that is nothing appertaining to them. A subject and a sovereign are different things.'

All reports show the executioner was very experienced. Whilst his identity was hidden behind a mask, his skill

Charles I praying before his execution. (With kind permission of the Thomas Fisher Rare Book Library, Library of Toronto)

reduced possible candidates greatly. It is known that Richard Brandon, the official hangman of London, was approached but refused. However, some reports maintain he admitted it had been him on his deathbed years later. Others were suspected but never charged, including Gunning, Daybourne, Bickerstaffe, two brothers named Walker, and William Hewlett, the latter having already been convicted of regicide after the Restoration.

At the Restoration of the Monarchy everyone concerned with this court and subsequent events was denounced. It was probably around this time that it was first mooted that John Bradshaw, as

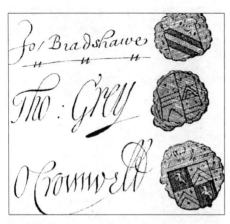

The signature of 'Bradshawe' on the death sentence of Charles I.

head of the court, effectively invented regicide. Although he was dead, as were the other two men on the bench (Oliver Cromwell and Henry Ireton), all three bodies were exhumed on 30 January 1661, exactly twelve years to the day after the king was executed. In a very public display of retribution, three dead men were hung in chains all day on the gallows at Tyburn. As the sun dropped below the horizon all three were beheaded, the bodies thrown into a pit and the heads displayed on pikes outside Westminster Hall.

Family notes suggest they may have got the wrong man, for his son, James Bradshaw, claimed to have already moved his father's remains and had them reburied on the island of Jamaica.

The spot on the hill was said to have been marked by a cannon and today there is a Gun Hill southwest of the port of Falmouth, Jamaica. However, this alternate version does seem rather convenient and was probably written after the exhumation and 'execution'.

Just ten days after regicide was invented, the *Eikon Basilike, The Pourtrature of His Majestie in His Solitudes and Sufferings* was published. It purported to be the spiritual biography of Charles I and is written in the form of a diary with prayers and thoughts. Within, the king forgives his executioners but defends and justifies royalty. It has never been proved that Charles wrote it: indeed, following the Restoration of Monarchy the Bishop of Worcester, John Gauden, claimed to have written it. Jeremy Taylor, a Church of England cleric, is said to have revised the original work and changed its original title of *Suspina Regalia*, the 'Royal Sighs'.

In October of this year John Milton published *Eikonoklastes*, 'the breaker of the icon', and in it defends the execution of the king. This book is a direct answer to *Eikon Basilike*, seen as a work of Royalist propaganda. Milton is best known for his poetry but was also a man of letters and a civil servant in the Commonwealth of England under Oliver Cromwell.

TORTURED BY A TRAITOR

The Terrible Story of Titus Oates

ACCORDING TO LONDONER Titus Oates, the year 1680 saw a Catholic conspiracy to assassinate the newly restored monarch – King Charles II was in mortal danger. Except that it was completely untrue. Oates, by clever manipulation of the facts behind a series of real events, created anti-Catholic hysteria throughout the land. For three years he managed to spin his web of lies until his massive deception was revealed; his conviction for perjury was inevitable. However, it was too late to help at least fifteen men who had already been executed for their supposed crimes.

Titus Oates had in fact already been shown to be a liar. His education was a disaster, being thrown out of both the Cambridge colleges he attended, yet he still managed to be appointed vicar of Bobbing in Kent. Around this time he accused a schoolmaster in Hastings of sodomy, which was found to be untrue: Titus was found guilty of perjury and gaoled. Yet he escaped and fled to London, where he found a job as chaplain on a ship in the English Navy. Here, ironically, Oates was accused of the same offence – that of sodomy – but

managed to escape prosecution as he was a man of cloth.

Back in Stafford, the central figure in the drama that was about to ensue was one Stephen Dugdale. Not exactly the most influential of figures, he managed to carve a significant niche for himself in history through his association with Oates. Dugdale had been in the employ of the Aston family of Tixhall Hall. As steward to Walter Aston, 2nd Lord Aston of Forfar, he had access to the cash box and managed to embezzle his employer out of a lot of money – and also to cheat the workers of a portion of their wages.

As soon as Dugdale realised he had been found out he fled, only to be captured by soldiers who were already lying in wait along the road. He was taken to Stafford's North Gate and interrogated by none other than Titus Oates himself. Unsubstantiated reports speak of the bag of gold still being in Dugdale's hand: his greed refused to allow him to relinquish what had taken him a good time to purloin. For three or four days Dugdale was imprisoned and forced to endure the horrendous conditions of this House of Correction.

The gatehouse is all that survives of Tixhall House.

The House of Correction was supposed to be a lesser evil than gaol, created in Tudor times to quite literally 'correct' the errors of those guilty of lesser crimes. However, at least until the prison reformers took an interest, condition inside were still vile, and corruption rife. Whilst we do not know specifics in the case of Stephen Dugdale, doubtless the corrupt Oates will have used every trick in his considerable experience to get exactly what he wanted.

Faced with such horrors, Dugdale broke. When he emerged he was nothing more than a puppet, obeying Oates' every command. In return for his release, Stephen Dugdale had sworn an oath stating he had overheard his master, the Catholic Lord Aston, plotting to kill the king. This was, of course, a complete fabrication but one which saw Dugdale's release and the start of a campaign around Stafford which saw any number of men arrested without warning.

Lord Aston himself was taken to London where he was thrown in the Tower. Several others were incarcerated in Stafford Gaol: a Mr Peters, of whom little else is known; a man called Cotton, evidently a priest; and one George Hobson, a well-known tenant of Lord Stafford and a personal friend of Lord Aston. As with the rest of the nation, now everyone eyed one another with the utmost suspicion. None had any cause to do so but, having placed the seed of an idea in their heads, rumours of the plot grew completely out of control.

Dugdale was soon producing 'evidence' to prove the guilt of others. His testimony alone sent three men to the scaffold in a single day: Father Gaven, a Mr Atkins, and one Andrew Bromwich. Atkins cheated the executioner, for he died in prison soon after the trial and avoided the awful death which awaited the other two.

Hanging at this time was a slow process of strangulation. Yet before they breathed their last the accused were cut down and, with the sharpest and largest of blades, the body was quartered. The two-pronged flesh fork was then employed to lift the still-steaming remains into cauldrons containing heated oil or tar. It is hard to visualise this awful scene. For those present, closing their eyes would have been of little help as they would still have been able to smell the acrid smoke, the pungent aroma of scorched flesh, and the nauseating stench of internal organs and guts roasting.

Still the bodies were not laid to rest, for their punishments forbade burial in consecrated ground. Often interred at crossroads – and pinned with a stake in the grave to prevent them from haunting those who had brought them to justice (or in this case injustice) – some were hung in a gibbet as a warning to others. The gibbet would have seen the body reassembled and covered with pitch so

COMETS AND CROWN JEWELS

Comets have long been considered unlucky, and this year saw the discovery of what became known as the Great Comet. It earned this name for its very long tail which, at its brightest, could be seen during the day. However, it is for the distinction of being the first comet to be discovered by telescope that astronomers remember it today. (Another excellent display was given by Donati's Comet in 1857, after another tragedy, this time at a local farm. The Northern Lights were also visible at least this far south that year – unlike the solar eclipse which, like the 1999 event, remained hidden behind cloud for most observers.)

Thomas Blood died this year, the man whose name will live on as the only fellow ever to steal the Crown Jewels from the Tower of London. At the time of his death he had been released on bail, owing the Duke of Buckingham £10,000 following a lawsuit issued against him. Some months later his body is thought to have been exhumed to ensure this renowned prankster had not faked his own death to avoid paying up!

that, as the flesh rotted away, the basic skeletal shape remained recognisable as an infinitely more effective deterrent.

Eventually Oates's reign of terror came to an end. Dugdale's perjury went a large way to undoing his partner in crime, for it was shown in court that his evidence was a fabrication, and he had attempted to bribe others to give evidence supporting his lies. Oates was found guilty and sent to prison, with the added punishment of a public flogging through the streets of London on five consecutive days each year. Amazingly he was later pardoned and even given an annual pension of £260.

Dugdale was never even brought to trial but released on bail in 1681. He died in March 1863, almost penniless and a habitual drunkard. A contemporary report prepared for Secretary of State Leoline Jenkins gave Dugdale's death as a result of drink. By now Dugdale was living a vagabond lifestyle, any evidence he was called upon to give dismissed as the ravings of a madman. He spent most of his time in a seeming state of terror,

in particular convinced a stranger he met at the Three Tuns in Charing Cross was Viscount Stafford himself, or at least his ghost, come back to exact retribution on Dugdale. Along with another of Oates' puppets, one Edward Turberville, drink completely took over Dugdale's life, 'delirium tremens and imagined spectres' haunting him to the very end.

His final hours were spent fighting off these imaginary phantoms, and he died a most miserable death.

Titus Oates in the pillory.

AD 1742

HORRORS OF THE WORKHOUSE

IN DECEMBER 1735, leading townsfolk met to solve the problem of the increasing number of poor in Stafford. At the meeting, all present agreed the major problem was not the begging in itself but that these members of the poor contributed nothing positive to Stafford. The twenty-first century solution would be very different to that of 1735 – the workhouse.

Ten men were appointed to cost the building of the new workhouse where the schoolmaster's house stood in the churchyard of St Mary's. It took another three years before work could begin. The catalyst was the £100 gift given by Viscount Chetwynd which kick-started the conversion of existing buildings (rather than demolishing those already standing and building anew). There were six chambers where the inmates would lodge, a hall used principally as a place of work, a kitchen, a pantry, cellar space also used for storage, a washhouse and a vegetable garden.

It is estimated there were some 350 operational workhouses in Britain by the time the Stafford establishment was open for business. They had begun in Tudor times as a way of providing food

and shelter for the unemployed. The situation was created by the most famous Tudor monarch of them all: Henry VIII's Dissolution of the Monasteries put an end to centuries of the church taking care of the needy.

By 1742 the workhouse was up and running, teething problems had been ironed out and officers appointed, entrusted with the day to day running of the place. While a warden runs a prison, a workhouse is under the watchful eye of a master. The doors first opened under Master John Hill who received an annual salary of £15 for himself and his wife, with the added bonus of twelve tons of coal mined at a nearby colliery. As with a prison, those sent to the workhouse were forced to follow a strict set of rules. Yet, unlike prisoners, the work done was first and foremost intended to benefit the inmates.

Some were sick and, not needing surgery, simply required nursing back to health with other inmates acting as nurses in house. Others were farmed out to perform necessary tasks in the big wide world. While they returned to the workhouse every night they were permitted to retain half of their earnings, giving them a start on the road back to independence.

Children were put to work spinning and knitting but were also taught to read. However, while education began at three years of age, by the time they saw five they were working, and by nine their education was completed. School began at 7 a.m. in summer, an hour later in winter for under-fives, and two hours earlier for older children who also had a job to do.

While those working outside the workhouse were allowed to come and go they had to return every night. Anyone found outside the area of the complex would face strict disciplinary measures, seeing an end to privileges, until they were deemed to have repaid the investment in them by the master of the workhouse and his staff. Church on Sunday was obligatory for all who could walk. No loitering or excessive drink was permitted or, once again, punishment would be meted out.

A more familiar regulation concerned smoking, which was completely banned within the buildings although tobacco products were permitted in the gardens. Those creating a disturbance, showing bad temper, and cursing or swearing, particularly around the sick, were denied meals to give them time to reflect on their unacceptable behaviour.

No fires were to be lit without express permission of the master, who would ensure the allowance of 12 tons was purchased at the correct season (i.e. when coal prices were at their lowest). The sick and infirm would be allowed fires at the discretion of the nursing staff, as would those charged with doing the laundry. To further save on the

An example of the inside of the workhouse.

heating none of the poor were permitted to be up after 8 p.m. in the winter and an hour later in summer. Furthermore, all candles were to be out by 9 p.m. with both servants and family in bed by that time, save for the nurses.

This rule was not always obeyed. On the night of the 15/16 May 1901, eleven people were sleeping in the infirmary block of Stafford Workhouse. Shortly before 2 a.m. the general alarm was raised by one Nurse Langtree when, as she was walking along a corridor, she heard the cook crying out, 'Fire!' She attempted to reach the poor trapped woman but was beaten back by the smoke and flames. Were it not for Nurse Langtree's bravery and quick thinking, the casualty list would have been far greater that night. First she roused the inmates of her ward and organised their safe escape; then she woke three women and allowed them to reach safety with their babies. Now she turned her attention to the fire, turning on the hose and holding back the flames until relieved by the master and matron of the workhouse. Her actions undoubtedly

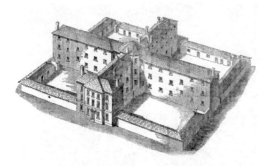

The standard design of the workhouse by Sampson Kempthorne.

spared the lives of many of the 260 inmates in the main block. The only fatalities were those people trapped in the wing beyond the ward where Nurse Langtree was working. Here were the cooks' room, and two wards, six bodies in the first and four in the other. Investigations revealed these last four would probably have survived – for there was little evidence of fire or smoke damage here – had they simply stayed low to the floor, below the level of the fumes and gases.

Not all inmates were repatriated into society. For some the trust shown in them presented them with easy opportunities to become thieves. Anyone found to have taken or embezzled money, linen, woollens, food, etc., would be summarily sent to either the House of Correction or possibly straight to Stafford Gaol.

Not that theft was by any means the worst of the crimes. A young woman of nineteen, who had returned to her native Staffordshire from the capital, was deemed to be too ill to be allowed to return to society; she was instead taken to the workhouse. Here a young girl of just seven years tended to her needs. Astonishingly, this situation was allowed to continue after the woman asked the little girl what happened to those who committed murder. Clearly, all was not well – a suspicion borne out inside of forty-eight hours, when the woman took a knife to the little girl's throat, severing her head.

In December 1839 Anne Wycherley, a twenty-eight-year-old mother of two, left the workhouse at Drayton with her two children: Anne, aged three, and Jane, just twelve months. A witness spoke of how she saw Wycherley go to a field belonging to one Mr Butler that same afternoon, where she flung the elder child into a pit. A second individual, a man with whom the witness was well acquainted, then threw several stones down that same pit. Three hours later, Wycherley and her surviving daughter called at the home of Sarah Newbroke, who lived some 2 miles from the scene of the murder. They arranged for young Jane to be nursed by Sarah for two shillings per week. Sarah shared some of her food with the mother and allowed her to rest, for she looked tired and worn. She enquired if she had any more children, and Wycherley replied she had had another who had died and was buried at the workhouse. This explained why, when the two bundles of clothing she left with Jane were examined, one was found to contain shoes and stockings for a three-year-old. On Christmas Eve a local constable recovered the poor child from the pit. The official reason given for death was drowning: water at the bottom of the pit had obviously finished what the fall and the stoning could not. Wycherley was subsequently arrested, tried and hanged the following year. She was judged to be perfectly sane at the time of the murder.

In 1845 one Thomas Rochell, along with his wife and two children, was given thirty-five shillings by a famiy member to travel, by train, from the London workhouse to the home of his family in Penkridge. He was unable to support his family at the time, owing to a diseased foot. After staying with his family for four or five days, the group travelled on, in a cart, to Haughton and applied for acceptance to the Stafford Workhouse. Refusal at Haughton meant he had no alternative but to try again at Stafford, where the family were accepted but as paupers of Haughton. When surgeons examined the foot of Mr Rochell they concluded the situation was now so bad as to warrant amputation, not just of the foot but of the whole leg. To add insult to permanent injury, the poor man then had to endure court proceedings as Haughton and Stafford argued over which of them should foot the bill (so to speak).

In 1847 a report suggested Stafford Workhouse was particularly prone to a 'low form of typhus' which they knew as 'Irish Fever', as it seemed to affect only those from Ireland and their nurses, with some 300 cases recorded.

The causes were thought to be various, although one observer was keen to point out that, prior to laying down upon the straw beds for the night, twenty were seen 'scratching in unison'.

Nearly 100 years later, in 1857, a report appeared that revealed another aspect of life in the workhouse. *Idiotic, insane and imbecile inmates of the nation's workhouses* were the theme of a report by Lord Shaftesbury released this year. It showed how 7,555 such inmates had been found in England and Wales, of which 239 were to be found in the county of Staffordshire, with seven male and twelve female inhabitants at Stafford. The two women to every one man ratio was seen throughout the country and, while no explanation for the difference in the apparent sanity of the genders was offered, this peer of the realm did point out the numbers were not spread evenly throughout the land. He added that those in rural areas were statistically more inclined to be declared *non compos mentis* than those in 'populous localities'. Furthermore, this was particularly true in hilly parts of the country!

Others left in a coffin. A strict procedure was laid out in the case of death.

English astronomer Edmund Halley was born in this year. His name remains one of the most famous in his field, as it is also the name of the most famous comet. He predicted the return of Halley's Comet after noticing the return of a comet every seventy-six years and suspecting (correctly) that it was the same body. Less well known was the diving bell which enabled himself and his men to spend ninety minutes on the bed of the Thames 60ft below the surface. The air was replenished by barrels weighted and dropped to the bottom. While the men were perfectly happy spending this time underwater, it was not practical for salvaging or working as it was too heavy for the men to move.

Immediately upon the death of an inmate a nurse should go to purchase a coffin. No more than six shillings should be spent on such for an adult, or half that for a child. The corpse should then be washed and placed in the coffin, the whole being taken to a place of rest awaiting collection. Clothes of the deceased were to be recycled by laundering and mending, and taken to the store room awaiting another owner of similar size.

Any nurse found to be benefitting from the death of the sick would soon find themselves bound for the House of Correction. This was also true of any entrusted with specific tasks in the workhouse: any neglect or failure to discharge their duties in an acceptable manner and they would be behind bars at either the gaol or House of Correction. Nurses received thruppence per week for performing their duties (they did work longer hours); kitchen staff earned a penny, tuppence, or thruppence depending upon their duties. But the master also kept an eye on their spending. Should he decide they were spending their money unwisely, they would soon find they had no money to spend – wisely or otherwise!

In 1838 a new workhouse was constructed on Marston Road. The architect was Thomas Trubshaw, the design based on the plans of Sampson Kempthorne (who produced the basic cruciform model for the Poor Law Commissioners three years earlier). The earlier workhouse housed an average of thirty-two of the poor; its replacement saw an increase in that number of at least 50 per cent.

Guardians and the Poor Law were still recognised until, little by little, they were removed between 1929 and the new Welfare State officially beginning in 1951.

AD 1772

LEECHES AND THE CROOKED KNIFE

Life and Death in Stafford General Infirmary

WHILST IT COULD never be said the level of medical care was anything but basic in the late eighteenth century, it was none-theless available. Over a number of years the need for a more permanent solution had been recognised and by 1765 steps were finally being taken to ensure a fully operating infirmary existed in Stafford.

Already some £600 had been bequeathed by men of the town, when fund raising began in earnest. Initially premises were sought to house this venture, rather than spending money on a purpose-built centre. A meeting of such dignitaries as the Bishop of Lichfield and Coventry, Lord Stamford, local dignitaries and benefactors was held in the Grand Jury room of the Town Hall. Here their attention was focused on Foregate Street where a number of indi-viduals had offered their premises at a low rent. Within a year these three prop-erties, along with two more, were being refitted and three doctors, Campbell, Hall and Withering, appointed as physicians.

Dr Erasmus Darwin was appointed surgeon-extraordinary here in 1783 and was to remain so until 1801, the year before his death. Darwin is of course a famous name in scientific circles; indeed, Erasmus was the grandfather of the more famous Charles. Another grandson, Sir Francis Galton, was a cele-brated polymath who can claim to have produced the first ever weather map among his numerous achievements. Erasmus was also related, by marriage, to the famous potter Josiah Wedgwood and a founding member of the Lunar Society of Birmingham, a meeting of some of the greatest minds of pioneering industrials, philosophers and men of science of the day.

Before long it was realised there had been a serious underestimation of the town's health needs and another meeting was convened. A meeting at the inn at Wolseley Bridge saw most of the original board present. Soon they emerged with an agreement to build an infirmary capable of holding eighty beds, with a budget of £2,866. Thanks to charitable donations, fund-raising sermons, and gifts from numerous sources, the infirmary was operational in 1772.

Annual reports were issued, showing the infirmary was efficient and well capable of tending to the sick of

Stafford and surrounding areas. While the pages of these documents would be considered quite unremarkable, the same is not true for the front cover. Each report was rather lavishly embellished by a wooden engraving of the building. Yet while this is undoubtedly the infirmary, the engraving does not depict a single chimney when there were clearly several.

Of course, these were enlightened times. Medical treatments were far in advance of two centuries earlier, when diagnosing involved tasting urine, treatment invariably employed leeches, and surgery was undertaken by barbers. This was 1772 and the leech was able to return to its natural life, for medicine had made the creature redundant with the introduction of the artificial leech. This may have terrified the patient more than the natural blood-sucker. Effectively a metal sawn-off bicycle pump with cutting blades, this did exactly what its namesake did – sucked the blood right out of the patient.

The centuries-old practice of blood-letting was one thing these enlightened Georgians had not abandoned. It was generally believed that evil spirits and excessive pressures were the main causes of ill health: thus to remove body fluids made perfect sense. Not that the doctors stopped at blood. Inducing vomiting, urination, and bowel movements by any means possible could only be beneficial. Or so it was thought.

This was also the first time that forceps were employed in childbirth. Not overly different from those we see today, they appeared at virtually the same time as male midwives. It is widely believed they were created to appear more professional in an area where female midwives were clearly more knowledgeable.

We can only wonder if the jugum (another type of clamp or forcep) was ever seen at the Stafford General Infirmary. Men said to be exhibiting anxiety, tiredness, and irritability were sometimes diagnosed as suffering from 'spermatorrhea'. This was the result of masturbating, something said to be at least as devastating as smallpox, for releasing sperm was blamed for causing weakness, mental problems, epilepsy, hearing loss and, of course, the inevitable vision problems. However, wearing the jugum would prevent such from happening.

When all else failed, doctors had no choice but to resort to surgery – including amputation. Doctors will have consulted the printed matter of the day and found such wondrous advice as 'checking the calendar before operating'. It was a well-known fact that the extremes of heat and cold in summer and winter could make operating problematic; much better to amputate in spring and autumn. It is also suggested the flesh be removed with a 'crooked knife', actually a hooked blade, as it

South-west along Foregate Street with Stafford General Infirmary on the left. (Photograph with the kind permission of Cliff Homer)

James Brindley died this year, having lived most of his fifty-six years at nearby Leek in Staffordshire. The famous engineer, best remembered for his canals, was attended by Erasmus Darwin, later to work at the Stafford General Infirmary, when complaining of a chill after being caught in a torrential downpour while surveying a new branch of the Trent and Mersey Canal. It was Darwin who had diagnosed him as suffering from diabetes the previous year.

makes for a much easier cut, the bones then being sawn before the skin was used to seal the stump.

French Pox would certainly have been treated at the infirmary, for this was how syphilis was known at the end of the eighteenth century. For the Francophiles there were alternative names such as lues, bad blood, Naples disease, and Spanish disease.

Other problems treated at the infirmary would be recognised but not by eighteenth-century terminology. For example, today lethargy would be seen as a symptom rather than an illness, but in 1772 the patient would be comatose! What we know as diphtheria was described as 'malignant sore throat'. Children would doubtless have been admitted with croup. Although we would possibly recognise the difficulty in breathing and the associated cough, reading the notes and finding 'rising of the lights' might be mystifying.

One of the most common treatments would have been the cataplasm, which

Surgery in the eighteenth century had made great advances. Note the man on the left has what appears to be a cigarette in his mouth and the man standing is holding a pipe!

sounds horrendous but is actually only a poultice. The screw was certainly known by Archimedes, but for the doctors at the infirmary 'screws' was what we would know as rheumatism. A stroke was referred to as 'softening of the brain'. Certain to induce panic among the community would be the mention of wool sorters' disease, although we would know this as anthrax (a disease, spread by cattle, which attacks the lungs and skin).

AD 1784

HORRORS OF THE PRISON HOUSE

IN **PREPARING A** report on the nation's prisons, John Howard visited the town in 1784. Howard was born on 2 September 1726 in London but soon moved to Bedfordshire, a county with which he was associated for the remainder of his life. After a sickly childhood, adequate education and a less than successful apprenticeship to a grocer to learn business acumen, his father died – leaving him with a sizeable inheritance but still no direction in life.

Howard set off on a 'grand tour', taking in much of Europe from 1748. After another bout of illness he set off on his travels again in 1755. (In the meantime, he had married the nurse who tended to him during the early 1750s. The marriage may not have been an overly happy one, however, for he gave away all her possessions when she died, after they had been married for just three years. This may not seem quite such a tragedy when we learn she was over sixty years of age at the time of her marriage. This was no pleasure trip: he was headed for Portugal and determined to assist in alleviating the suffering in the aftermath of the Lisbon earthquake. Howard never arrived. His vessel, the *Hanover*, was captured by French privateers and he found himself imprisoned at Brest until eventually exchanged for a French officer held captive by the British.

From the moment of his release he showed a great interest in prisons. Yet it was not until he was appointed High

Stafford Gaol's prisoners received Brownie points (literally) for good behaviour yet punishment was severe. All too often the male inmates, irrespective of age, were summoned to the prison yard to find a man tethered to the flogging post at the waist. He was stripped, his hands bound to the feet to expose the back. A practised hand delivered thirty-six lashes with the cat. Thereafter the man was kept in solitary, in a room of total darkness, for three days on a diet of bread and water.

THE PRISONERS ARE ESCAPING!

Eleven years later, in August 1795, a most daring gaol break was discovered at Stafford. Inmates were awoken by the sound of sawing and raised the alarm. None escaped: indeed, those who were aiding the would-be prison breakers also joined their friends inside. An astonishing array of keys was found upon their persons, while inside a prisoner had hidden numerous articles under his bed, and a grappling hook with a rope attached was later found buried in the yard.

Sheriff of Bedfordshire in 1773 that he actively proposed prison reforms, his first official statement in giving evidence to a House of Commons' select committee the following year. By the time of his death in 1790 he had made four tours of British prisons, as many of those in Europe, and even crossed the Atlantic. He calculated he had travelled around 60,000 miles just visiting prisons.

Here we shall concentrate on his third tour, during which he paid a second visit to Stafford Gaol and the County Bridewell. When publishing *An Account of the Prisons and Houses of Correction in the Oxford Circuit*, Howard makes comparisons with his previous visit and notes 'no alteration' – a term only employed when he considered the conditions unacceptable.

Firstly Howard comments on the County Bridewell, a building where offenders were held awaiting trial and sentencing, but effectively also used to house those found guilty of petty crime when there was no room at the gaol. Whilst he sees no improvement from his earlier visit, he does concede the place is kept clean and prisoners are not in irons. Howard is not happy with bedding, which was merely straw changed every

fortnight, and voices the same dietary concerns raised at the gaol.

For every prisoner the gaol could claim two shillings and sixpence per week to cover the cost of their lodgings. Of this amount two shillings was for food and included fifteen penny loaves. Whilst Howard found the bread to be of good quality and weight, the remaining

Awful and gloomy conditions of the exercise yard – itself a rare treat for prisoners.

nine pence purchased 2lbs of cheese – which he considered entirely inappropriate – and could be spent on milk, oatmeal, potatoes and other vegetables, and enable them to have a hot meal most days.

During the day those allowed a little freedom were brought to the day room. This was considered entirely inadequate, being far too small to accommodate the crowd of prisoners, both male and female, brought here daily. Examining the dungeon for male prisoners, he counted fifty-two in chains. Each had a space averaging just 14in wide and the heat was unbearable even for the visitor. Moisture was running down the walls, said to be from the breath of the prisoners themselves; this problem could be solved by adequate ventilation. He notes seven prisoners died the previous year from what was then known as gaol fever – although we would refer to it as typhus – and a direct result of the conditions.

Fresh air was something also missing in the room directly above the male dungeon. Here the free ward, as it was known, was effectively the debtor's prison. Conditions were no better here, with nine of thirteen held here dying the previous year. The gloom could have been alleviated by a window and yet the only one had been bricked up, after an inmate had attempted to escape through it, leaving the room far too dark and humid.

Any inmates exhibiting signs of ill health were forced to remain in the communal cells, for there was no infirmary. Hygiene was non-existent, a bath being out of the question as there was no facility for bathing. An Act of Parliament, designed to see to the well-being of prisoners, should have been displayed but was conspicuous by its absence.

Above the women's dungeon, itself less cramped simply because female prisoners were less numerous, was a similar room where debtors were held. The room was light and well ventilated, had a high ceiling and a hearth for a fire in winter. However, no prisoners were ever kept here: the room was used to store, of all things, the gaoler's lumber. When Howard enquired as to why this place was not used to reduce the overcrowding, he was informed the room was insecure. Howard insisted it was more than suitable for holding criminals not deemed dangerous or perhaps where the sick and dying could be placed, for there were certainly enough in this category to warrant the allocation of space.

HOW MANY RIOTERS CAN YOU FIT IN ONE CELL?

In August of 1842 workers in Stafford were demonstrating against the lack of job opportunities. The town's local government brought in Colonel Monkton to lead the Staffordshire Yeomanry against the rioters and restore peace. He succeeded within days, arresting seventy individuals and throwing them in Stafford Gaol. This brought the total number of inmates to 708, more than there had ever been – or ever would be again.

ON THIS YEAR

Bales of cotton from America arrived in this country for the first time this year. The skills and technologies based on the wool trade proved invaluable when it came to producing cotton cloth.

The Treaty of Paris was signed on 14 January this year, marking the official end of the American Revolutionary War and the end of colonial rule in the United States.

Plans for a new gaol in the county were awaiting final approval and yet, as a prisoner reformer, Howard was also interested in reducing the number of potential criminals, for it is much harder to put a villain back on the straight and narrow than to convince a law-abiding citizen not to fall into a life of crime. It was with this in mind that Howard took the magistrates of Stafford to task.

He noted that every window in the building faced out to the street. This enabled prisoners to see freedom on the other side of the gates but also offered them an excellent view of three ale houses in three adjacent buildings directly opposite those gates. One of these, which sadly he does not name, had its licence withdrawn after it was discovered it had been harbouring a gang of criminals. When they were finally brought to justice, many being executed for their crimes, a collective sigh of relief was heard across the town. Yet within weeks of his arrival the licence had been renewed by magistrates and already suspected criminals were known to be meeting there.

Howard went on to suggest the magistrates were 'so dreadfully supine and timid' as to be dominated by the clerks of the town. Howard intimated these clerks had their own interests at heart, either in having a finger in the proverbial criminal pie or of receiving a back-hander to turn a blind eye to nefarious dealings which transpired here (and possibly both). Thus licences were granted for establishments where ale was little more than a cover for crime, sin and vice.

It must be said John Howard had a point. Today it is normal for an establishment to have one big room, whereas a couple of generations ago a good sized public house would boast a bar, a lounge, a smoke room, and a gents-only room together with an outdoor (that's beer 'to go' in the modern vernacular). Thus it is impossible to see the justification in granting licences to sell alcohol at three adjoining establishments.

THE FARMER'S PLOT

WHEN THE HARVEST failed in 1794, few but the farmers felt the initial pinch. Yet by the following summer the story was very different, for not only Stafford but the whole nation was running short of the most basic of food sources – wheat.

Markets, in cities across the land, saw prices double within days and continue to climb. Imports could not alleviate the problem. Britain was at war with France, itself in the midst of a revolution, while the weather had also affected harvests across Europe. As wheat prices increased so did flour prices and, most importantly for the man in the street, the staple food of bread.

Starvation was the inevitable result. With many already struggling to feed themselves and their families, it was inevitable that answers would soon be demanded. Unfortunately, the hungry men and women of Stafford took their anger out on the millers and the bakers who were suffering equally with the rise in prices of this crop. A gang of miners, suspecting farmers were hoarding wheat to jack up prices even further, stormed farms and broke open barns. Of course they found their suspicions were unfounded: all they had succeeded in doing was causing criminal damage to property. Worst of all, they had gained access to farms by trampling the new crop of wheat which would have been harvested in the autumn of 1795.

Fortunately Stafford had always benefitted from the generosity of its landed gentry. Historically this county town had never been among the wealthiest

ON THIS YEAR

Born this year was poet John Keats. The same year also saw the death of perhaps the most famous potter ever, Josiah Wedgwood, who was sixty-three years of age.

The 21 November this year featured an earthquake in Stafford. At five minutes to seven a group of gentlemen were surprised to see the glasses on the table overturned and smashed. We must assume, by the mention of glasses on the table, that this was five minutes to seven in the evening.

The Royal Navy made the use of lemon juice mandatory on all their vessels to prevent scurvy.

The Broad Eye Windmill still stands, albeit without sails, today. Local mills were attacked in this era.

in the country; thus, it was the norm for the 'haves' to help out those less fortunate. Several leading figures organised a meeting at the Swan in June to attempt to alleviate these problems. They emerged having organised monies to be distributed to farmers and millers to subsidise the production of flour and thus bring affordable bread to the poorest families of Stafford. Special mention should be made in respect of Abraham Ward, the man responsible for the town mill, who undertook to grind wheat for free when approached by those who so desperately needed the help.

Sadly this did not prevent the problem growing increasingly worse during July. Then in August imported wheat, landed at Liverpool, was brought along the canals of England in two horse-drawn barges to nearby Radford where they were moored overnight. On the morning of the 4 August a large number of men from Stafford appeared on the towpath refusing to allow this vital commodity to leave the area.

On hearing of the troubles the Volunteer Cavalry were summoned. Under the leadership of John Sparrow they came to the hill overlooking the site of the dispute. Commanding his men to remain, Sparrow dismounted and walked alone and unarmed to face the angry men on the towpath. By now it was apparent these supplies were earmarked for the Black Country. Sparrow made them see the error of stealing from other hungry mouths simply to feed their own and convinced them to accompany him back to Stafford.

Sparrow further promised that subscriptions would be raised immediately upon their return to relieve the people and bring them supplies of flour and/or bread. While the magistrates supported him, they did add the condition that anyone found guilty of rioting or looting would lose such privileges. Should any doubt their resolve, the magistrates reinforced their determination to enforce the rules by fining bakers who had already broken regulations.

Meanwhile, John Wright and Francis Brookes, two wealthy men of Stafford, realised the problem of flour and bread shortages would recur with increasing frequency. The growth of the population, mainly down to the expansion of the shoe trade bringing workers in from afar, would result in a serious shortfall in milling capacity. This could

A wheel from the town mill: the mill leat still flows feet from here.

What was to become the town mill saw early construction problems. An insufficient fall of water meant the mill had to be wind powered and thus a higher tower would be required to ensure wind could reach the sails. Within weeks it became clear these problems were insurmountable and the two men returned to the council with news that they had persuaded William Fieldhouse, owner of the High House, to cede more land and an old barn next to the mill site. This proved sufficient leverage to get a revised lease of 500 years with no increase in rent. The mill was operational within eighteen months.

The new mill was a tower design with a rotating cap. The tower construction soared to 56ft, with the sails reaching much higher. The sails were attached to the cap, as was the vane. Together they turned independently of the tower, always keeping the sails facing the wind and optimising the potential wind power.

only be addressed before the problem arose. Hence mercer John Wright and solicitor Francis Brookes, who was on the verge of retirement as town clerk, easily convinced the council to grant a ninety-nine year lease on three gardens and adjoining waste ground near Doxey Bridge for the nominal rent of five shillings per annum.

AD 1833

THE BODY IN THE GAOL

FOLLOWING THE ANATOMY Act of the 1 August 1832, the dissection of those sentenced to execution was permitted. The very same act also declared that the bodies of every executed criminal thereafter belonged to the Crown and therefore could only be buried within the confines of the prison walls.

At Stafford an area was allocated on the northern side, near the solitary confinement cells. The trampled soil here gave no indication of anything different to the rest of the open yard. In the ground the body was wrapped in a sack; above, a stone slab – the only sign of what lay beneath. On the slab was inscribed 'Executed for Murder', with a name, age, and the date that the sentence was carried out. A grave in unconsecrated ground, the grave of a murderer.

Clerk of the parish of Ranton, Joseph Evans was known as much for one of his daughters, twenty-year-old Mary Evans, whose beauty ensured she stood out in any crowd, as for his own achievements. For several weeks in 1833 she had been 'keeping company' (as was the phrase of the time) with Richard Tomlinson. Mary was not living with her father but staying at a cottage owned by Thomas Tildesley, her sister's husband. On Sundays they were in the habit of visiting another sister at Knightley, and 15 December 1833 was no different.

The second sister was married to a John Hatchett. The Knightley couple

A LOAD OF ROT!

In the earliest days lime was added to prison graves as it was thought to hasten decay, but this was stopped when it was realised that it actually helped preserve the corpse!

Prior to burial in prison grounds, those executed for murder after the passing of the Anatomy Act were no longer returned to relatives for burial but sent for dissection. Fights between the family and the anatomists were by no means uncommon.

Ranton church, near to where the body was found.

made them welcome and allowed Richard and Mary to share a room, having been told they were married. However, this particular Sunday Mary Evans was not so enamoured with her man – indeed, she constantly accused him of the theft of a watch and some sovereigns. He denied the accusation and countered with comments damning her morals, suggesting the time she spent talking to a waggoner on the way there was excessive and her manner overly friendly.

Mrs Hatchett suggested her sister visit 'a conjuror' at High Ercall who would tell her what had become of her possessions. Hence Monday morning saw Mr Hatchett accompanying his sister-in-law and Tomlinson as they began their journey to High Ercall. Clearly the latter was not anxious to make this unexpected detour, for he began to complain that he 'felt ill'. Tomlinson's constant complaints about what was very obviously a feigned indisposition became quite tiresome, and Mr Hatchett soon made his excuses and returned home.

Later that day Mary Evans' body was recovered in a ditch beneath an oak tree, only 200 yards from Ranton's church. She was found face down in water twice its normal depth of 2.5in, as her body had acted as a dam to raise the level. Her bonnet and her cloak showed signs of a struggle, while a large stone near the body was later identified as the likely weapon and cause of the head injury which was undoubtedly the reason for her death.

The prime, indeed only, suspect was Tomlinson and a search was instigated for a stout and rather short man of twenty-two years, with an excessively plump face, and overly large round head. However, they did not have to look far, for he was at the beer shop of a man called Phillips, the husband of Tomlinson's sister. Two hours after the still-warm body of the victim was pulled from the ditch, the murderer was in custody.

Yet Tomlinson had not been alone during those two hours but talking openly to a farmer named Betteley. Their conversation was given as evidence at the trial, since Betteley thought Tomlinson so calm that he could not have killed anyone. However, Betteley soon learned the body had been discovered exactly where Tomlinson said he had last seen Mary Evans.

Held at Gnosall awaiting trial, Tomlinson was visited by magistrate Revd W.H.C. Lloyd of Norbury. Here he admitted his guilt, saying, 'I did it and am ready to die for it. I only wish I may be laid by her side.'

Lloyd had the prisoner's confession recorded by a Mr Smallwood and endorsed as a legal document. Oddly, it was never brought as evidence at the trial, although details of Tomlinson's childhood were.

Mary had taunted him the day she died, Tomlinson said, saying his mother was a murderess and his father in gaol. This was not quite true: his father was long dead, as was his mother. She died of a long-time liver complaint when awaiting trial for the murder of her husband ten years earlier. When his father's body had been exhumed, traces of arsenic were found in the stomach of the man, who had been in his seventies. His wife, some twenty years his junior, was already bed-ridden but insisted the children bring their father's food to her before serving it.

Such a poor start to life, but one which improved when he was taken into the home of some relatives. He even joined the army. However, Tomlinson's short

military career came to an abrupt end when he was dismissed for some minor misdemeanour. His father's will left him the tidy sum of £250, although he got through this rather quickly – particularly at the beer house where he was lodging in the village of Ranton.

The seven-hour inquest, surely a mere formality, ended at 10 p.m. with a verdict of 'wilful murder'. Tomlinson spent his entire time in gaol in prayer, confessing to his excessive drunkenness, breaking of the Sabbath, and the getting in with bad company which had led to his actions. He agreed to the sentence. At 8 a.m. on Wednesday, 19 March 1834, the sentence was carried out.

Although he had expressed a wish to be laid with the victim, this was never to be realised. Thus the first man to be buried inside Stafford Gaol is marked by a stone

Now a modern housing estate, the body was found in a ditch by an oak tree, both long gone.

slab reading: 'Richard Tomlinson, aged 23, Executed for Murder, 19 March 1834'.

HANGED, HANGED, HANGED AND HANGED

There are no less than four ways of hanging which, over the years, have been employed by the executioner:

WILLIAM MARWOOD
FROM THE WAX MODEL
IN MADAME TUSSAUD'S

William Marwood, the inventor of the Long Drop.

- ☠ **The Long Drop** – first seen in Britain in 1872. A table of the weight and height of the individual calculated the length of slack rope required for an efficient execution. It was designed to ensure the neck was broken and death came quickly – but not as quickly as decapitation if the drop was too long – and thus considered more humane.
- ☠ **The Standard Drop** – another scientific table introduced in 1866 and also designed to break the neck. Was replaced by the Long Drop quite quickly when it was found a couple of necks refused to snap.
- ☠ **The Short Drop** – used before 1850, the idea was simply to stand the individual on a movable object – a cart or horse, or sometimes a ladder. As it was taken away, the condemned person died by strangulation, typically taking some ten to twenty minutes.
- ☠ **Suspension** – as the name implies, the weight of the body tightens the noose and the individual is strangled. Often struggles were reported as minimal, as the tightening noose prevented blood flowing to the brain. The Royal Navy hoisted mutineers up from the deck of the ship with a rope passed over the yardarm.

STRUCK WITH A STONE

The Strange Case of Mary Kearnes

I N MAY OF this year a very sorry sight was helped into court to give evidence. Mrs Mary Kearnes appeared very ill, clearly but little recovered from the injuries she had sustained some fourteen days previously.

Also in court was the man accused of wounding her, Mr John Maines. As the case unfolded the events of that Saturday evening, just a little over a fortnight earlier, were revealed. First to give evidence was the victim. It was shortly after midnight when, having heard an exchange between her husband, Farrell Kearnes, and the accused, Mary went to her window. She and her husband kept a lodging house in which Maines had been a guest for some time. Maines, clearly fuelled by drink, was spoiling for a fight with Mr Kearnes, but had been told,

'Johnny, I'll not fight you tonight, stop until Monday morning.'

Upon cross-examination Mary admitted she had been drinking but, like her husband, could 'never' be described as drunk. Below she saw John Maines, who clearly was the worse for drink and had awakened them with his shouting. She had called out to Maines, telling him, 'Go away, you old cuckold.' In response, she said, Maines had picked up a large stone and thrown it at her.

Farrell Kearnes' evidence corroborated his wife's. He had heard her 'cuckold comment', adding she then cried out, 'Oh John Maines, you have murdered me!' as the stone struck her. She collapsed and was caught by her husband. However, he told the court that he did not see Maines throw the

---

Medical treatment may not have been too advanced in the nineteenth century, but for Henry Shelley of Hopton anything would have been better than what he received.

At the inquest, his family were blamed for hastening his death by procrastinating when it came to summoning the doctor; because they did, a case of bronchial infection proved his downfall. The official verdict? 'Died by the Visitation of God.'

The outside view of the Guildhall and Market Place in the nineteenth century.

The Guildhall still maintains an old cell where prisoners were held awaiting trial.

stone which had caused her injuries. If it seems odd that Mr Kearnes did not see Maines throw the stone – after all, it was a sizable lump of rock and would have had to have been thrown with some force – the next witnesses called complicated things even further.

He was one Thomas Merricks, a cordwainer who knew Maines (at least by sight). Merricks, awoken by the noise at such a late hour, came downstairs from his bed to the street. His home was sixty yards from the scene of the furore, yet still he was able to see and hear the accused being called a 'cuckold' – and clearly this was the voice of a woman. Here the stories differed, for neither Mary nor Farrell Kearnes told of a delay between the cuckold insult and the

throwing of the stone, yet Merricks was adamant he heard an angry exchange of words between the two, both the accused and the defendant using 'much bad language'. Merricks then led Maines into his home to calm down. Two witnesses – a joiner by the name of George Adams, and another man named Isaac Mason – were inside the house with Maines when they heard the woman cry out, 'Oh John Maines, you have murdered me!' Shortly afterwards a constable came to arrest Maines, saying he had thrown a stone and badly injured Mrs Kearnes. Both witnesses insisted that this was not possible: he had neither picked up nor thrown anything. However, they did say they saw a man in 'a hairy cap' and, while they did not see him hurl the object, perhaps he was the person responsible for the throwing of the stone?

Other witnesses offered nothing new and eventually the case was dismissed; John Maines was allowed to go free. Nobody else was ever brought to trial and no record of either husband or wife is ever found at this address again.

There are three possible solutions to this strange affair: the witnesses' stories

EVENTS OF THE YEAR

Christmas 1836 saw the death of one of the servants of William Cornwell, County Hall Keeper. Jane Barlow died a few hours after she ran across the Butter Market to the Guildhall – she had hoped to inform him that she was on fire! Her clothes had caught light when she was cleaning the hot ashes from the hearth, one of a worrying number of similar accidents around this time.

Also this year, Charles Darwin, grandson of former Stafford surgeon Erasmus Darwin, landed at Sydney, another stage on his voyage of discovery aboard the *Beagle* which did much to help him publish his book on evolution.

were fabricated in order to protect Maines, the true culprit (though it is hard to see the motive for this); a mysterious unknown man had been at the scene of the crime that night; or there was some undisclosed trouble in the Kearnes' house.

One further piece of evidence may provide the answer, for three people stated Mary Kearnes threw the word 'cuckold' at Maines. Little used today, a 'cuckold' refers specifically to a man whose wife is guilty of adultery. Why was Maines intent on fighting Mr Kearnes? And why was the latter, by his wife's testament, trying to calm the situation and inviting the angry man to spend another two

nights under their roof? Maybe Mr Kearnes had a bigger role in this than it seems: had Mr Kearnes perhaps had an affair with Mr Maines' wife? That would explain why the two men were shouting at each other through the window. It also makes it easier to imagine what could have happened to explain Mrs Kearnes' injuries if the lodger had *not* thrown a stone at her – perhaps the wife had been struck by her own husband, and she simply put the blame on the other man? After all, no stone was ever produced in court.

The only thing that is certain is that at least one of those present that night lied to hide the truth.

AD 1838

THE BASILISK

ABASILISK IS a mythical creature. This king of the serpent's name comes from the Greek and means 'little king'; it is said to possess the power to kill with a single glance and leaves a wide trail of deadly venom in its wake. Stafford does not have a basilisk today but in 1838 it did have a *Basilisk* which was to prove equally as deadly.

On the afternoon of the 11 November 1838 the *Basilisk* made the news. On the Grand Junction Railway at Stafford, at almost exactly 3 p.m., the *Basilisk* was the name of the steam locomotive which had just been repaired at Stafford and was heading back to its base at Liverpool. Barely 1 mile to the north, the train met a very heavy train travelling from Manchester. With the south-bound train already running some thirty minutes late, the *Basilisk* gave way and began to reverse back to Stafford as instructed by the signalmen.

Back at Stafford the engine came into sight and a signal bell was sounded by signalman Edward Owens. On the footplate of the *Basilisk*, driver John Howard and fireman John Hunt were heading back to a secure siding to thus

An example of a mid-nineteenth century steam locomotive, this is the most famous of them all – George Stephenson's Rocket.

allow the safe passage of the Manchester train. On hearing the signal William Dearn emerged from the engine house.

William Dearn had previously been a successful and highly respected local butcher but a series of misfortunes meant he had fallen on hard times. Hence this quiet and extremely well-mannered man accepted a job on the railway. Despite the task of lubricating the wheels of rolling stock being among the lowliest of positions he had been very grateful to his new employers for offering him the chance to feed and clothe his wife and their eight children.

Women received the vote for the first time this year, also giving them the chance to run for office. However, this was only in the four Pitcairn Islands in the Pacific Ocean, a 'group' spread over hundreds of square miles of ocean yet only measuring 18 square miles of land. While it would be almost another ninety years before full women's suffrage was won in Britain, oddly Pitcairn was granted such on the very day it became a Crown Colony.

Meanwhile, Queen Victoria's coronation took place at Westminster Abbey in June. She lived to the age of eighty-one, reigned for sixty-three years, had nine children (six of which pre-deceased her), was a widow at forty-three, and survived at least seven genuine assassination attempts.

Coming out of the engine house he was in no great rush. There was nothing in sight and he had no notion that anything other than regular services were operating. He certainly was not expecting the *Basilisk* and was blissfully unaware of any danger as he walked between the rails. However, he was alone in not seeing the danger.

First signalman Edward Owens called out to him but his warning was drowned out by the general hubbub around the junction. Others did hear and emphasised the warning. At the subsequent inquest,

aptly held at the Grand Junction Inn, it was stated that at least three, and possibly more, stationary engines blew their whistles but still he paid no heed to them. By now even those on the footplate of the *Basilisk* were alerted to the situation and did everything possible to stop their locomotive whilst yelling at Dearn to get off the line – but it was too late. By the time Dearn realised his peril the engine was almost upon him. At the moment of impact the *Basilisk* was travelling at just 7 miles per hour, but this was still too fast for the unfortunate Dearn.

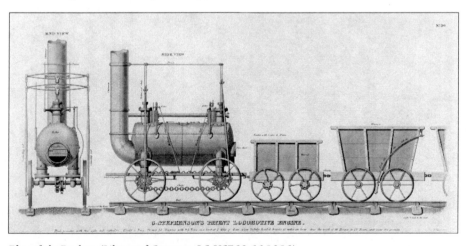

Plan of the Rocket. *(Library of Congress, LC-USZ62-110386)*

The locomotive knocked him down and then the rearmost wheel became the instrument of his death. The wheels crossed the body from the right hip. The right arm was crushed, bone fragments protruding through the sleeve of the jacket. Ribs were broken and dislocated, with the chest cavity so distorted his lungs had been forced out through the hole in the side of his chest. Finally, the wheels crossed the neck, severing the head from the body save for a small flap of skin at the nape of the neck.

Afterwards the sickening sight turned even the stoutest stomach but particularly affected two men: nothing could persuade signalman Edward Owens to identify his colleague afterwards; neither could fireman John Hunt, whose own brother had met a similar fate some years earlier.

THE WENCH IS DEAD

The Tragical Case of Christina Collins

ONE OF THE best known murders in the county of Staffordshire took place on 17 June 1839. Later that day, the still-warm corpse of Christina Collins was dragged from the Trent and Mersey Canal just outside Rugeley.

Over 170 years later the climb leading up from the tow path is still known as the Bloody Steps – the legend has it that they were stained red by the poor woman's remains. These steps are cut from sandstone, a soft rock which erodes easily. Hence these are unlikely to be the original steps, and yet they still, it is said, ooze blood at times (usually a prelude to a sighting of the tragic victim's ghost, which has often been reported along the tow path).

Much has been written about her end but little about the rest of her life. Born in Nottinghamshire in 1801, the daughter of unsuccessful inventor Alfred Brown, she had received a good education and was first married to Scotsman Thomas Ingleby, who earned his living as an illusionist. His repertoire included beheading a chicken and bringing it back to life, smashing and repairing a watch, and eating six items of cutlery.

He also found time to pen a book on his trade, *Ingleby's Whole Art of Legerdemain*, published in 1815.

Thomas Ingleby was very much older than his wife and, when he died in 1832, she was a penniless, childless widow alone in Ireland. She moved back to England and in 1838 married again. While her first marriage saw more excitement on stage than off it, her second was passionate and a true romance. Robert Collins, a hostler, was unable to find work in Liverpool, so he left his wife there to earn a meagre living as a seamstress, before sending her one guinea (equal to around two weeks wages) for her to join him.

Later investigations showed she had been making her way from Liverpool to London to be reunited with her new

> Written by Colin Dexter, the Inspector Morse story produced for television as *The Wench is Dead* was based on the circumstances surrounding the murder of Christina Collins.

husband. She managed to get a lift from three men on a barge.

As the *Chronicles of Crime* has it:

> Deceased entered the boat at Preston Brook ... The boat proceeded thence [from Stoke-on-Trent] to Stone, where it arrived at about eight the same evening. At Stone the deceased complained to a check clerk of the canal company that the prisoners were becoming inflamed with liquor, and said, that she was afraid of going on the boat with them. The deceased, however, went on with the boat from Stone, having got out there and walked by the towing-path side some distance. About dusk they were met by another boat, when some gross language in reference to the deceased was used by one of the prisoners, and a short time afterwards they were again met, and the prisoners used expressions in reference to their intentions as to the deceased of too disgusting a nature for publication.

About twelve o'clock on Sunday night the boat arrived at a place called Hoo-mill-lock. By the side of the lock was a house occupied by the lock-keeper and his wife. They were both awoke at midnight by loud cries of distress, and immediately opened their bed-room window, when they perceived the boat in question in the lock. The deceased was in the boat, and upon the prisoners being asked who she was, they replied that she was a passenger and that her husband was in the boat with her.

Proceeding a little further, they came to a place called Colwick-lock, and after they quitted that place the

An idyllic view of the Trent and Mersey Canal near where Christina Collins met her awful fate.

deceased was not seen alive. The body of the deceased was found in the canal at a part of the canal known as Brindley's-bank, between Colwick-lock and Rugeley, and about three miles from the former place.

The men tried to claim that the woman had jumped overboard and drowned herself, but it was obvious to all that they had dumped her body in the canal. The report contained a rather sad coda: 'The cabin of the boat was searched, and in it were found the bonnet and shoes of the deceased, the bonnet being very much crushed.'

The woman's body was examined, and found to bear evidence of 'great barbarity'. Eventually three men were brought to trial: James Owen, George Thomas (also known as Dobbell), and William Ellis. Owen's cellmate came forward to say that on Sunday 21 July the prisoner had spent the evening discussing their crimes. Owen told the man that he and his two friends had 'some whiskey on board the boat, which they stole and drank; [and] that they then used the woman roughly, and she got out and walked on the towing-path.' The *Chronicles of Crime* concludes that 'the greater part of the statement is unfit for publication; but it amounted to an admission, that the capital offence ... had been committed upon the unfortunate woman by all three of the prisoners, and that her struggles to escape were so great that, in their belief, she had died, and they then threw her overboard.' This was later proved to be untrue: the injured woman was still alive when thrown overboard, and had drowned in the murky waters of the canal.

All three freely admitted most of their living came from theft, never passing up an opportunity, with other boats proving particularly rewarding. As if public opinion was not already heavily against them, they then added that none of them had ever spent a single hour in church during their adult lives.

It took nearly a year to get them to the gallows, principally because the evidence against all three was largely circumstantial. On the eve of their execution not a room, nor a bed, was to be had in the area, such were the numbers who came to witness the sentence being carried out.

THE POWER OF LOVE

In this year a woman was discovered hiding in a London prison for men, having pleaded guilty to a crime she almost certainly did not commit. Her gender was revealed when a fellow inmate noticed her menstruating. All this just so she could be closer to the man she loved!

A fourth individual, a teenager by the name of Musson, had been found aboard the boat. However, he was cleared and released. Yet it was a small boat, most of the space taken up by the cargo. Even if Musson had not seen anything, he must surely have heard something. However, there is no record of him giving evidence against his fellow crewmen, nor was his innocence ever questioned (at least, not openly).

At an early hour the chaplain, the Revd Edward Rathbone, and the governor visited them and urged them to repent. Owen and Thomas stated they had nothing more to add; Ellis did not speak. Owen and Thomas then read from the Bible while Ellis, being illiterate, simply stood nearby and listened. As the clergy went through the funeral service the occasional tremor in their voices revealed that no one had been unaffected emotionally by this ghastly murder.

Just before they were due to be taken to the scaffold, a message came from Her Majesty: Ellis had had his sentence temporarily reprieved; confirmation also came from Lord Normanby. When the other two discovered Ellis was not to die that day, Owen wept, while Thomas said, 'Bill, if you get off let this be a warning to you as long as you live', which seems to suggest Thomas had no doubt as to Ellis's guilt. Eventually Ellis was transported for the rest of his life.

Having said their goodbyes to their colleague, the executioner bound their hands and the knell of a bell heralded their final journey. As the chaplain read the funeral service the procession walked to the drop. An estimated 10,000 people watched from every available spot; windows, walls, trees, roofs, no spaces were unfilled as they ascended the steps without assistance or hesitation. A noose was placed around their necks and as the chaplain spoke the words, 'In the midst of life, we are in death', the bolt was drawn back.

The silence was broken only by the odd gasp from some of the women. Two strong men convulsed on the end of the ropes for some time, being cut down an hour later. This was the signal for the crowds to disperse quietly and with due solemnity.

Two slabs in the yard read: 'James Owen, aged 39, Executed for Murder, 11th April 1840' and 'George Thomas, aged 27, Executed for Murder, 11th April 1840'.

Christine Collins's memorial, paid for by the people of Rugeley, horrified by her death.

A memorial stone stands in the grounds of the parish church at Rugeley. This was erected some years later, paid for by donations from locals. The inscription reads: 'To the memory of Christina Collins, wife of Robert Collins, London, who having been most barbarously treated was found dead in the canal in this parish on June 17th 1839, aged 37 years. This stone is erected by some individuals of the Parish of Rugeley in commiseration of the end of this unhappy woman.'

FALLING FOWLES OF THE FIDDLER

or, Who Killed Martha Keeling?

MARTHA KEELING WAS a well-known figure. She had worked all her life, almost always as a cook, saving every penny she could. Now in her fifties she had realised her ambition, saving enough money to open an eating house and taking in lodgers.

In March there was but a single person lodging here, one Matthew Fowles. This was a time when anything out of the normal was quickly noticed and when Martha had not opened her shop at the usual time that morning neighbours took it upon themselves to investigate. It was 10:30 a.m. when clock and watchmaker John Beeland and a colleague made their way through the premises to Martha's room. Here she was found on the bed, her lifeless body, quite cold, indicating she had been dead for some time. It was later discovered she had been strangled.

A box was found beside the bed. In here she had kept her valuables and some money. The box had been forced open and the contents were missing. Sharp-eyed neighbours spotted two possible clues. Firstly there was a silver spoon found by the body on her bed: this probably came from the box and had been dropped by whomsoever had stolen the contents. Furthermore, a fowl and a ham had been seen hanging in the window of the shop by more than one person and had been there between the hours of 10 p.m. and 11 p.m. on the previous evening. Both pieces of meat had vanished next morning. With Fowles the only lodger, and he no longer to be found, he instantly became the number-one suspect.

Severe sentences were often passed in the nineteenth century. In November an employee of the Post Office was brought to trial for stealing a penny. He asked to change his plea to guilty, but the court refused. At twenty-nine years of age, William Henry Moore fainted when he was sentenced to transportation for the rest of his natural life.

Enquiries revealed something of his recent movements. For example, a tailor told the court that he had sold a coat to Fowles at 4 a.m. that Wednesday morning – a garment he had shown interest in just twelve hours earlier when, 'penniless', he certainly could not afford to buy it.

Next the trail took them to the railway station, where a witness reported seeing a man answering Fowles' description eating the meat of a fowl and counting money of gold, silver and copper. Here the suspect had made enquiries about trains to Hartford, buying a ticket there and getting on the 6 a.m. service (where he would change at Birmingham before continuing on to Hartford, near Northwich in Cheshire).

Fowles had previously lived at Hartford. When the investigating officers visited his earlier known address they found him there. He denied ever having stayed with Martha Keeling, nor even having visited the town. Yet he was found with rings, a brooch and money amounting to £1 10s 6d in silver and a further sixpence-ha'penny in copper coins. He was asked to explain these items, but the people he said had given them to him knew nothing about it when asked. Evidence was mounting against him. The silver spoon found next to the body, missed by the murderer and thief since it was in the folds of her apron, matched others discovered in Fowles' possession by police officer Michael Madden. The new coat was found in his room, along with a cap, two cotton handkerchiefs, a comb and a knife – all clearly recently purchased.

An artist's impression of Jack Ketch. His incompetence as an executioner was part of the reason for his name becoming generic for every executioner who followed.

Fowles later admitted he had been lodging with Martha, but said that there had been others in the house. When shown this was unlikely as only two beds in the house were made up (one for the victim and another for the murderer), he claimed he had shared his room with 'a fiddler'. This mysterious fiddler had strangled poor Martha and robbed her. Subsequently he shared the loot with Fowles in order to keep him silent, even agreeing he could keep both the fowl and the ham in order to seal the deal.

Charged and brought to trial, his seat in the box would still have been warm when the jury returned after just two minutes' deliberation. Despite his continued insistence of his innocence, it was inevitable Matthew Fowles was pronounced guilty. After sleeping soundly he awoke on Saturday 3 April and ate a hearty breakfast. Prison guards later said he appeared to pray silently but they could not be certain.

At 8:05 a.m., in front of a crowd of almost 3,000, Fowles ascended the scaffolding and the noose was placed around his neck. When the bolt was drawn back the condemned man dropped and death came almost instantly.

AD 1842

RABIES COMES TO STAFFORDSHIRE

ONE BENEFIT OF living on an island is the natural barrier it provides. Customs and immigration officials must delight in how easy their job is compared to other nations, forced to create man-made barriers. It is impossible to thus create a barrier to every creature: many will pass under or over the wall or fence. This is not the case with an island.

Our story starts in March of this year. Two men from Stafford had travelled to Birmingham, seeking work. The first sign of trouble came following their return to Stafford. On Sunday 4 September, James Shenton, a seventeen-year-old shoemaker, was admitted to the County General Infirmary suffering from breathing problems. His condition deteriorated rapidly. Within hours he was convulsing, and soon after refusing to take his medicine or any liquid. The resident surgeon, Mr Crump, had his suspicions and asked if Shenton had been bitten recently. Both he and his relatives denied this, and yet the slightest breeze brought increasingly more violent convulsions and it came as no real surprise to Mr Crump when his patient died the next day.

Yet before the post mortem had been performed on Shenton, the infirmary had another patient. George Peach, at thirty-two somewhat older than his friend, was later described as 'an intimate companion' of James Shenton. Furthermore he was also employed in the shoe trade and, as it later transpired, had been the other man who had travelled to Birmingham to seek work.

When Peach was admitted he began to exhibit similar symptoms but was attended by a different surgeon, a Mr Masten. By Tuesday morning Peach was unable to swallow the coffee or indeed the liquor brought to him and Mr Masten also raised the question of a bite – an allegation which was, once again, denied.

Within seventy-two hours of his admittance to the infirmary Peach was also dead. After complaining of a pain from his left shoulder to the neck, on the Wednesday his convulsions were so violent that he was seen jumping out of bed. Any noise, drink or even the gentlest breeze would make him worse, while the sight of certain objects seemed to have a similarly violent affect.

Rowlandson's print of a 'mad dog in the coffee house', showing the terror caused by rabies – or the fear of rabies – in earlier times.

Nurses reported that, at 3 a.m. on the Thursday, he was found out of bed and pounding his head on the stone floor, apparently in an attempt to take his own life. When approached he tried to bite them; he also bit the bed and anything else which came within reach. At just after 4 p.m. on Thursday afternoon, George Peach's torture ended.

Shortly after their death it was discovered that both men had a bite mark on the hand. It seems during their time in Birmingham they had adopted a dog. Described at the time as a 'Blenheim', this will have been the most common colouring of what is normally referred to as the Cavalier King Charles Spaniel. It was also discovered there was a third victim, for three months earlier a nephew of Peach, whom they had met in Birmingham, had died following identical symptoms.

The dog, which had disappeared two days after they had taken it in, was never heard of again. As an epidemic of rabies was not reported it seems the creature did not live long enough to pass this terrible disease on to many, if any, others.

Rabies is a Latin word meaning 'madness'. This is thought to have come from a Proto-Indo-European word related to the Sanskrit *rabhas*, meaning 'to do violence'. Of the 55,000 cases reported annually, 97 per cent are a result of dog bites. The rabies virus can infect any warm-blooded animal, although no bird has ever been shown to be infected (other than those used in experiments).

AD 1855

POST MORTEM

Three of Stafford's Weirdest Deaths Revealed

THE FIRST RECORD of this office is found in 1194. However, his job was very different to either the modern coroner or that of the middle of the nineteenth century. Originally the coroner's duties were, as their job title suggested, to resolve pleas made to the Crown. In 1855, as today, their principle task is to decide whether unnatural and unexplained deaths required investigation.

What may seem an odd evolution of duties is easy to understand when we explain why the office existed in the first place: suicides, shipwrecks, treasure troves, etc., were all to be investigated, but with the main concern of ensuring the remaining lands, monies and goods of such were forfeited and given to the Crown.

For the coroner the year of 1855 would have been an interesting and unusual one which saw three cases requiring his attention. In February he was called to examine the case of eighty-five year-old Thomas Prinhold.

For some time he had been resident at the workhouse in Stone. However, the old man had recently become increasingly violent. He was judged to be insane,

and it was decided to transfer him to the County Asylum in Stafford. The year was only days old when, with no chaise or similarly closed carriage available for the journey, an open phaeton was driven to Stone to transfer old Thomas.

January is statistically the coldest month and this year did not disappoint. It was bitterly cold, no conditions in which a man of such advanced years, without even the good sense to try to keep warm, should be riding in the open. When he arrived at the asylum he collapsed. He died of exposure the next morning, and was buried that day.

Mr Wilkes, the superintendent of the asylum, correctly reported the details to both the Lunacy Commissioners and the Secretary of State. For the next five or six weeks the three men corresponded regularly until, one day in February, it was agreed to call an inquest into Thomas Prinhold's death and the coroner was summoned. With the body exhumed an inquest was held at the Trumpet Inn, Stafford.

The verdict of death due to exposure went unchanged. However, the powers available to the coroner can be seen in his recommendations following the

STAFFORD IN 1855

—∞∞∞—

In May workers from Stafford bound for the Paris Exhibition were supplied with passports free of charge to enable them to live and work in France for as long as it took to erect and dismantle the exhibitors' stands.

The end of the Siege of Sebastopol, now known as Sevastopol, was announced in Stafford on 10 September this year. This important victory of the Crimean War had lasted almost exactly a year to the day and marked the end of the conflict. When the townsfolk heard the news they understandably celebrated. And what celebrations! The usual rejoicing and drinking was to be expected, yet the crowds also fired cannon, lit bonfires, bell-ringers sounded the bells of St Mary's, and even the Stafford Band played on and on until 2 a.m!

The effects of the war were however still being felt at the end of the year. With Christmas just three days away, the local press carried the news of the opening of the soup kitchen. This sixteenth-century building was to contain an eating house where Victorians could purchase a ticket for thruppence. The ticket entitled the purchaser to a meal as usual, yet with a portion of the money distributed to the poor during winter months to help alleviate the usual shortages and those caused by the Crimean War. As residents will know, it is still open today.

—∞∞∞—

inquest. Thereafter no lunatics were to be held in the workhouse but only in the asylum – albeit adding the words 'if at all possible' to leave a loophole – as this very often seemed to result in fatalities. Furthermore, the authorities, both at the workhouse and the asylum, were severely reprimanded, deemed culpable in this and many other cases, and warned as to their future conduct.

The coroner was summoned again in October. On the 11th of that month one Daniel Moores had been taken to the infirmary following an accident just outside Stafford railway station. His legs were crushed. The damage was great and both limbs were amputated below the knee. Despite receiving the best medical attention, he died the next day.

At the inquest a number of witnesses were produced, most of whom were travelling companions of Mr Moores.

Several work colleagues had purchased tickets to travel together that day and were seated in the same carriage when the whistle was heard and the train began to pull out of the station. It was then that the deceased put his head out of the open window, with the result that the hat he was wearing fell off. Witnesses described how he immediately opened the carriage door and descended the steps in order to retrieve his hat. The train was not moving quickly and it would have been a simple task to leave the train, recover the hat, and return to the carriage to continue the journey. Yet having reached the ground safely, he was suddenly pulled over when the steps of the next carriage caught in his coat pocket. With the train still moving, poor Daniel Moores was dragged under the next carriage, where the wheel passed over both legs at the ankles.

Today the coroner's court is held either at Victoria Square...

... or St Martin's Square.

With Moores the only person who could be held responsible for the incident, the coroner recorded a verdict of 'death by misadventure'.

A third and final example recalls a case put before the coroner just over forty-eight hours before the end of the year. Two days earlier a man had been found dead in his bed. Yet this man was known to be previously fit and well, and thus natural causes seemed most unlikely.

Opening the inquest, the coroner heard from the only witnesses available. These were all friends and colleagues of the deceased, military men having recently returned home after fighting for King and Country in the Crimea. Sent back to Stafford for some well-earned rest, these young men did what many would have done: they celebrated. Indeed, they all celebrated together at a local inn, not leaving until 6 a.m. the following morning, by which time they were very drunk.

Together they walked home to their lodgings where, for reasons never made clear, a fight ensued over – of all things – celery! One soldier aimed a blow at his colleague, who dodged the punch easily enough but in his drunken state fell heavily. All of them retired to their beds and nothing was heard until midday –

when the man who had fallen was found dead in his room. Whilst there was no external sign of injury, he had vomited over his chest, presumably as he slept.

Obviously the coroner was not convinced the soldiers had told the whole truth for his verdict was not accidental death. Here the assailant was charged with manslaughter and sent for trial. However, there was insufficient evidence to convict anyone, or even to show a crime had been committed, and the men were allowed to go free.

COFFINS AT NEW YEAR!

On New Year's Eve of 1755, a stone coffin was unearthed on Newport Road during building work. The top slab was broken and thus, with the weight involved, was impossible to move intact. Hence the two pieces of the lid were removed and revealed two skeletons within. Yet they did not last long enough to be investigated, for they crumbled as they were touched. Later it was announced that these were probably both female, a decision based entirely on this coffin dating from a time during the reign of Queen Anne (1702-14) when this was land belonging to a priory.

THE RUGELEY POISONER

William Palmer

WILLIAM PALMER WAS born in Rugeley in 1824. At the age of seventeen he went to study medicine in London, qualifying in 1846 whereupon he returned to his native Staffordshire. This was to mark the beginning of a trail of fatalities attributed to Dr William Palmer.

In the Lamb and Flag at Little Haywood, Palmer met George Abley, a plumber and glazier who boasted of his ability to hold his drink. It was inevitable someone would throw down the gauntlet to this challenge, although Abley would not live long enough to regret accepting Palmer's. Within an hour he had to be carried home and before morning George Abley was dead. Locals maintained something was afoot as Palmer had been seen to show great interest in the extremely attractive Mrs Abley.

He married local girl Ann Thornton in 1847 and in early 1849 his mother-in-law came to visit. She was known as a wealthy woman, having inherited £8,000 a few years earlier. Some of this money she had loaned to Palmer but he never repaid any, for two weeks later she was dead. The official verdict, from Dr Bamford, was apoplexy. Meanwhile,

Dr Palmer's feeling was one of disappointment when he discovered the size of the inheritance.

In 1850 Palmer's interest in betting on the horses resulted in him meeting Leonard Bladen. When Mrs Bladen learned of her husband's death, she was surprised to discover he had very little money on his person despite having won a large sum quite recently. The written records of her husband's bets were conspicuous by their absence.

Dr William Palmer sketched from life. (THP)

DEATH IN THE CRIMEA

———— ∞ ————

Stafford wasn't the only deadly place to be on this day. A report by Adjutant-General J.B. Bucknall Estcourt reported on casualties at the Battle of Inkerman, a famous engagement of the Crimean War. Together with 1,878 wounded, 645 were listed as missing or killed, split into officers, sergeants, drummers, and so-called 'rank and file'.

———— ∞ ————

Furthermore, Bladen died at Palmer's home, with the death certificate giving Palmer as 'present at death'. The cause of death was said to be an injury of the hip sustained some six months previously, resulting in an abscess in the pelvic region.

Even more shocking revelations were later discovered concerning the deaths of four of Palmer's five children. His eldest, also William Palmer, died in 1926 aged at least seventy-six. Yet all the other four children died well before their first birthday. While infant mortality rates were frighteningly high in the middle of the nineteenth century, that Elizabeth (two and a half months), Henry (one month), Frank (seven hours), and John (four days) all died as a result of 'convulsions' was questioned following his conviction.

By 1854 Palmer had amassed a great deal of debt. Then in 1854, having insured his wife's life to the value of £13,000, she apparently succumbed to the cholera epidemic sweeping the country. Again it was later suspected that his knowledge of medicine enabled him to bring about the appearance of cholera when he had actually poisoned her.

He was still in debt, for more than £20,000, when his brother Walter died in 1855. As with his late wife, Palmer had also taken out a large insurance sum on his sibling and the company refused to pay, instigating an enquiry into possible fraud. This also revealed a third insurance policy on George Bate, a farmer who had worked for William Palmer but briefly. To further complicate matters his housemaid, Elizabeth Thame, gave birth to a son in 1855, just one of what eventually emerged as numerous illegitimate children fathered by William Palmer.

It was when he took the life of John Cook that the law finally caught up with him. Cook had been a friend of Palmer for some time when they ended up at the Raven, a local pub, following a big win by Cook at the races. While Cook had won £3,000, Palmer had lost heavily on the same race, which would have put the killer in a bad temper – and also note how this situation is almost identical to the initial death. Their celebratory drink was marred by Cook reacting badly to a glass of brandy procured by Palmer. As Cook later told two friends, 'I believe that damn Palmer has been dosing me.' When the two men returned to Rugeley, Cook took lodgings at the Talbot Arms. Later these men took coffee together and Cook became ill. Then later, when Cook's legal representative sent him some soup to hasten his recovery, the patient's condition worsened. Furthermore it would be shown that the soup had come into the possession, albeit briefly, of Palmer when it was taken to the kitchen to be reheated. Here a kitchen maid, who had tasted the soup to ensure that it was warm enough, also fell ill soon after taking the meal to Cook.

Next day Palmer collected bets on Cook's behalf. It was later discovered he also purchased strychnine which he administered in two pills, with a later dosage of pills containing ammonia. Cook died in agony that night. When William Stephens, Cook's step-father, suspected Palmer's involvement he demanded an inquest. Palmer was observed trying to interfere with evidence during the post mortem. He sent a letter to the coroner suggesting a verdict of 'natural causes' and enclosed £10 for his trouble. Just to cover his tracks even further, Palmer paid post-master Samuel Cheshire to intercept correspondence addressed to the coroner. For this transgression he later served a two-year sentence.

Maybe all this was pointless as the coroner could not find any trace of poison. Yet, convinced Cook had been poisoned, he stated this as the likely cause of death. Despite the evidence being largely circumstantial, and mainly of his own doing, Palmer was arrested and charged with murder and also forgery. This second charge of forgery was based on statements by creditors that Palmer had been forging his mother's signature in order to pay his own debts. Again there was no physical evidence.

When it came to his trial it was argued local feeling would prejudice the outcome and thus the trial was moved to London. Already, such was the vast amount of evidence, Palmer had spent six months in Stafford Gaol during which time the bodies of his brother and wife had been exhumed and examined and the stories of the deaths of four of his children had been widely circulated. After this period of time it must have been quite a relief for him to enjoy a little freedom when he travelled to the capital.

Leaving Stafford on the last day of May via the railway station, he was accompanied by a prison warder and the Deputy-Governor. As was usual the prisoner was neither handcuffed nor chained. Entering the station's buffet he toasted his companions and joked with the barmaid, although it is fairly certain she had no idea of his identity.

If she was working thirteen days later when Palmer arrived back at the station she would certainly have been aware

The final resting place of John Parsons Cook, one of William Palmer's many victims.

this was the notorious Rugeley Poisoner. Found guilty and now firmly chained, it was midnight when he arrived back at Stafford, flanked by a Stafford superintendent and the governor of Newgate Prison. We will never know if she recognised the man, who had been in very different spirits a fortnight earlier.

Stafford Gaol held prisoners sentenced to death by hanging. Not all were murderers: there were also those found guilty of what we would see as much less serious crimes such as horse-stealing, sheep-stealing, cattle-stealing, house breaking, arson, attempted murder, highway robbery, assault and robbery, counterfeiting, and forgery. A report this year stated that of 107 publicly hanged at Stafford Gaol, only four were women.

The job of executioner was hardly a full-time position – even if everything from stealing sheep to arson, burglary, and even passing forged coin or paper money merited the death penalty. Hence they were also paid to administer other forms of punishment. One famous hangman from the nineteenth century, a man by the name of Calcraft who worked well into his sixties, boasted how he could, 'Lay the flesh open to the bone with a single stroke of the cat'. The thongs of the cat were loaded with lead pellets to cut the flesh ever deeper. Each stroke drew blood, which would dry on the leather thongs – certainly not acceptable to Health and Safety today!

Next morning the largest crowd ever to gather in the town assembled outside the gaol. Various estimates have been put on the numbers, ranging from 20,000 to as many as 30,000. A bell tolled in the tower of Christ Church, but little else could be heard accompanying Palmer to the gallows on the morning of 14 June 1856.

His family, still protesting his innocence, begged to be allowed to bury him but were denied his body. Palmer was interred in Stafford Gaol's chapel. Only his initials and prisoner number engraved upon the stone slab identified the Rugeley Poisoner. Even in the twenty-first century he remains the county's most notorious killer.

AD 1857

HISTORY'S DEADLIEST GAMBLES

JUST 1 MILE south of the town, at the end of Church Lane in Coppenhall, is Butterhill Farm. Today, when the wind is from a favourable direction, the sound of traffic on the M6 motorway can clearly be heard in the distance. Aircraft pass overhead and the occasional train add to the background noise every hour, both day and night.

However, it has not always been this way. In the middle of the nineteenth century, aside from the steam locomotives in the distance, only the occasional passing horse-drawn cart would intrude upon the sound of Mother Nature. On the farm the young Merricks family were going about their usual daily routine. A family of five, they had started their day very much as they had most mornings that summer. Before night fell that evening it would have been a day none of them would ever be able to forget.

Mr Merricks had left the home early as did any good farm labourer. His wife was just outside the back door, doing the family wash in a large tin bath or wooden half-barrel, helping the soap and water do their job by agitating the

Another accidental gun wound accounted for the death of Thomas Colclough, who died in Stafford Gaol in 1858 awaiting trial for stealing fowl. A post mortem report showed that he died from an abscess on the brain which, when examined, was found to be caused by a piece of metal imbedded within his head. This 1.5oz lump was identified as a piece of a gun barrel. It later transpired Colclough had overloaded his gun some fourteen months previously, resulting in the explosion bursting through the barrel and a piece lodging in his head. This was also evidence to show Colclough was poaching in April 1857. An official decision was reached that, owing to the perpetrator being unable to appear in court (he was dead!), all charges against him would be dropped. The local press carried the story of how the widow Colclough intended to use the dropping of the charges to bring about a compensation claim for wrongful arrest!

Above Butterhill Farm, Copenhall.

Right Copenhall Church seems certain to have held the funeral for the tragic twin.

contents with the washing dolly. Behind her their three children were playing in the kitchen. Young twin girls played quietly together, while their slightly older brother was off to one side.

Young Master Merricks had made a most fascinating discovery in the corner of the kitchen. He picked it up and, as he was examining it, it exploded – it was his father's gun. The loud bang brought Mrs Merricks racing into the room, where she saw the two girls. Emma Merricks was lying dead on the floor with her twin sister leaning over and peering inquisitively at the entry point made by the bullet, an almost bloodless hole just above the right ear.

The boy was so distressed he ran away and was not seen again until much later that day. By this time the distraught father had been found and had returned home to what remained of his family. He took the gun and broke it in two, throwing both pieces into a nearby pond.

STAFFORD'S OLDEST INHABITANTS

Victorian journalists had a very different view of life. Those at the *Staffordshire Advertiser* reported how four natives of the town, two brothers and their respective wives, had recently slept under the roof of one house. This was newsworthy as their combined ages totalled 300 years, an achievement for the time. However, twenty-first century headline writers would not have given the piece the title of 'FOUR PEOPLE STILL ALIVE!'

AD 1860

STRIKE!

DURING THE NINETEENTH century shoemaking was among the major employers in the town. Many worked from home, for the work was mostly done by hand. Workers owned their own set of tools, keeping them in excellent condition and guarding them well. Clearly this was a significant investment and without such they would be unable to work.

Thus when one Mr Singer made important improvements to the sewing machine the people of Stafford had good cause to be worried. A job they had done by hand all their lives could now be mechanised and production increased greatly. This was fine for those who could afford the new technology but for the rest it spelled financial disaster. The workers could see no alternative but to take strike action. This was not be a withdrawal of labour in the modern sense, but could indeed be seen as such in a very real sense – for they left Stafford in their droves. Stafford employers were at a loss to understand just why their workers refused to undergo minor retraining just to use a machine which would make their working lives much easier.

However, they were not the only ones to feel the impact. Far harder hit were the families of those men who had moved. The men found themselves work alright – lodgings were much easier to come by in those days – but the wage packets never found their way back to Stafford. Left without a breadwinner, Stafford suddenly found itself home to women and children who were rapidly descending into destitution. This was absolutely unacceptable, and led to a Stafford shoemaker complaining of how his former workers were 'taking the strike as an avenue to divorce'.

Not all shoemakers had deserted their hometown. Poaching was a common way to add to the meagre menus of the majority and, for those with the knowhow, their quarry could be sought directly. This left out the middle man, and the only expense was in time and trouble. Oswald Beeman had been adding to his table for years, meaning more of his hard-earned cash as a shoemaker could be spent at the local pub instead of the butcher. With the strike he saw the opportunity to fill his pockets and simply spent more time poaching.

One Thursday in May Beeman was in the grounds of Creswell Hall, his favourite hunting place. When he saw a keeper approaching he panicked and, as he attempted to unscrew his gun in order to hide the pieces in his voluminous pockets, managed to discharge it. Hit from point-blank range, the bones in his left leg were utterly shattered above the ankle. Rushed to the infirmary, he paid a high price for his illegal activities – for that leg was amputated at the knee. Perhaps this was considered to be adequate punishment, for there is no record of him ever being charged for his crimes.

Six months after the strike began to hit, one manufacturer called a meeting with his competitors. Something had to be done to encourage their workforce back to Stafford, otherwise not only would their families starve but they would soon be out of business. An agreement was reached whereby all would pay an extra penny on shoes and twice that amount on boots and welts if the men returned to work and accepted the new technology.

As the workers came home to Stafford the businesses were saved and wives and children were no longer forced to beg for food. While no companies went out of business as a direct result of the strike, it is impossible to gauge whether their action did lasting damage either to the town or the industry.

THE THINGS THEY WILL NICK!

Refrigerated vehicles were unheard of in this era, and the safest and surest means of getting fresh meat to the butcher was to make it walk there. The butcher had their own slaughterhouse and led the animals to their end by means of a halter. One butcher was perplexed when several of the halters disappeared over a number of nights. He instigated a search of the property and was stunned to discover them in the room of a servant. She had removed the ends and used them in place of metal hoops to fill out a very full, and quite weighty, skirt.

AD **1870**

FOUL STENCH

IN **THIS YEAR,** General Tom Thumb and his troupe gave two performances in Stafford at the end of his tour of Britain before returning to the USA. This was the stage name of Charles Sherwood Stratton, who made a living out of being 3ft 4in tall thanks to the famous showman P.T. Barnum – the two were related. This was stretching nepotism to the nth degree, as they were described as 'half fifth cousins, twice removed'.

Also this year, Manders' Exhibition of Wild Animals came to Stafford in June. This, the largest of the travelling menageries, featured specimens from around the world, including everything from 'the leviathan elephant to the pretty-feathered cockatoo'. These animals were said to have a collective value of some £50,000, the equivalent of around £4 million today.

A less entertaining meeting was held in the tour in this year too. The New Year was welcomed in by a special meeting of town councillors and local notables to address an increasingly serious problem – sewage.

Mr Ward, the borough surveyor, showed the planned redesigning of the sewage system to alleviate a continued problem in the area around Gaolgate Street and Greengate Street, beginning near the Dolphin Inn. While sewage currently exited at Eastgates, he proposed taking the sewage to the north of the town. Pipes would need to be laid from the Dolphin to Gaol Square and thereafter to the brook at Backwalls North. This would also involve reversing the direction of the brook, a simple enough task, taking the sewage away from the town. Mr Ward maintained the whole project could be accomplished for £235 to lay the pipes and another £40 to install a flushing tank.

Not all the commissioners present were overly enamoured by the design, the cost, or the idea. Several pointed out there was insufficient fall to the brook and the sewage would not drain at such an angle. A certain Mr Whalley was particularly vociferous as he questioned the need for such expense. Amusement ensued as he pointed out that there were numerous inhabitants of these streets who had attained great age and/or bulk despite the 'alleged unwholesome smells'.

Not everyone agreed with Mr Whalley – not only those who were forced to

Eastgate today.

Gaol Square now forms part of the new ring road.

live with the foul stench from the open sewers objected. Included in the letters page of the *Sentinel* was a complaint from one Benjamin Boodger. This businessman felt more than justified in writing to the local press as he was forced to visit on a weekly basis. One wonders how much influence his words had on the eventual decision when he penned:

When a bird fouls its nest, perhaps other linnets may remark on the impurity without giving offence to the interested. For my sins I am doomed to spend one night of every week in Stafford's polluted atmosphere, and a dire punishment it is. Offal-boiling, tallow-melting, gamy sewage, and a thousand stinks murder the sleep of unhappiness.

The problem was raised several times during the year. Meetings of the town council and also the improvement commissioners addressed and rejected the sewage question again and again. Finally the new sewage system was agreed by a vote of ten to four. Work began within a week and cost just £250, actually marginally less than the estimate at the beginning of the year. Further improvements in the system were planned but quickly abandoned when a Mr Spilsbury agreed to sell some of his land for the widening of the road. However, when he sent in his invoice charging an exorbitant five shillings a yard the plan for Tenter Banks was rapidly shelved.

However, this did not stop the complaints. In the appropriately named Tipping Street, fingers were pointed at the slaughterhouse belonging to Mr Bridgewood. The tanning yard belonging to the company known as Messrs Elley, Gibson and Woolley was blamed as the principal source of the problems of the drains at Forebridge and that of the Newport Road. Officers wrote to the offending companies and also allocated extra funds to the night scavenger. Employed to rid the streets of the worst of the rubbish, more money provided extra hands in the short term. It was expected that the winter weather would bring greater rainfall and provide sufficient water to flush the build-up from the unusually dry summer.

Administrators later admitted they were unaware that the extra monies allocated to clean up the streets did not realise a similar increase in the number of hours of work. This only became apparent when smallpox cases were reported in the town. Immediately the onus was placed upon the townsfolk

A much cleaner River Sow in the twenty-first century as it heads toward the age-old crossing point at the south of the town.

to clean up their acts and to clean and disinfect at every opportunity lest they too should become victims of this dreadful disease. As the death toll mounted, the town council resorted to distributing dilute carbolic acid via handcarts for use as a disinfectant.

AD **1887**

FIRE!

OCTOBER 1887 AND the new month was just over an hour old when a young man by the name of Coniffe smelt smoke. He was in the Elizabethan House in Gaolgate Street, even at the end of the nineteenth century one of the oldest buildings in Stafford.

Coniffe raised the alarm and within fifteen minutes the fire engine was on the scene. This creditable performance was rather marred by their inability to draw water from the manhole in Goal Square. On removing the cover they discovered mud had clogged the access point and it took a further thirty minutes before water could be pumped from here onto the fire. This proved to be a vital delay, a problem later resolved by regular inspection of these access points (which are still carried out to this day).

By 2:30 a.m. a witness is recorded as describing the fire as already a 'roaring furnace, the timbers blazing with incredible ferocity and the whole illuminating the sky with a sickening glare, seen for miles around'. Clearly the Victorian press chose their witnesses carefully to ensure a good command of the English language.

By now it was evident the fire was in danger of spreading. The work was further hampered by the gathering crowds and a shortage of volunteers. Even those who did offer to man the pumps did so only with the promise of a good supply of beer to quench their inevitable thirsts. Our reporter was again in full Victorian mode when taking great pains to point out the supply of beer was not requested by 'clergymen and several ladies'. At 3 a.m. the focus turned to nearby buildings, some of which were in very real danger of bursting into flames.

In a week the local press were describing this as 'the most serious disaster of its kind to befall the town'. Four shops and their contents were totally destroyed, and a fifth damaged so badly it had to be demolished. Undoubtedly the worst hit was the business of goldsmith Mr L.C. Mummery. However, in true British spirit this businessman took out an advertisement in the newspaper released just six days later. In it he thanked the people of Stafford for frequenting his shop at No. 1 Market Square for the previous twenty-five years and assured them he and his staff would continue to serve the town

*Market Square from
Gaolgate Street around
twenty years after the fire.*

Market Square, Stafford.

*Another view of Market
Square, probably from a little
earlier than the view above.*

from temporary premises at No. 16 Gaolgate Street, emphasising a more than adequate workshop had been set up in the rear for repairs.

Later, firemen complained that the jet of water could not reach the top of the building owing to a lack of water pressure. Other voices were soon raised against the fire-fighting resources, not only the equipment but also the inadequate water supplies. In particular, why had the water supply at the asylum drain been found to be dry? The press did point out that, despite failing equipment and inadequate water supply, the fire brigade were to be praised for their work that night.

The boys from the press were keen to lay blame on the local council. It was suggested that it had been common knowledge the fire-fighting equipment was out-dated and woefully inadequate, particularly in and around the Market Square. The mayor immediately launched an appeal for funds to purchase a new state-of-the-art fire engine. Within the first week £300 of the required £700 had been raised, although this soon slowed and the mayor resorted to pointing fingers at those who he thought should have contributed.

Firstly he cited the local insurance companies. If a brand new fire engine could be obtained this would surely reduce possible payouts. Thus the paltry £5 contributed by Equitable was laughable – and perhaps the other companies should be making more significant contributions. A week later he had turned his attention to the fire department, pointing out it was they who stood to benefit most by making their jobs very much easier. As a result two weeks later senior fire officers were in London watching the testing of a steam fire engine. It was eventually purchased and named *Elizabeth* after the mayor's wife.

Not a single life was lost, it was claimed. If true this would be remarkable, for at one point the whole of the town centre was under threat with the eventual damage bill given as £20,000 – or about £1.5 million today.

IN THIS YEAR

Queen Victoria was proclaimed Empress of India on 1 January, a title Prime Minister Benjamin Disraeli had encouraged her to accept. He had pushed an Act through both parliamentarian houses the previous year: always referred to as the Royal Titles Act, it should correctly be known as 'An Act to enable Her most Gracious Majesty to make an addition to the Royal Style and Titles appertaining to the Imperial Crown of the United Kingdom and its Dependencies'.

Britain's summer sporting calendar would be quite empty had it not been for two events this year. On 15 March the Marylebone Cricket Club played an Australian team at what is now recognised as cricket's first ever test match. Then, on 9 July, the All England Lawn Tennis and Croquet Club began what became an annual tournament at Wimbledon. Competitors served underarm in a fund-raising event designed solely to raise sufficient cash to purchase a pony-drawn roller for the croquet lawns.

AD 1889

THE SISTERS, THE BAKER AND THE SHOEMAKER

SATURDAY 2 JUNE must have started off as a normal day for two sisters. Both were living at No. 16 County Road with their respective husbands.

This was the home of twenty-three year-old William Faulkner, a shoemaker employed by Peach and Co., his wife and their two children. Six months earlier, the wife's sister had moved into their home, having married twenty-eight-year-old Richard Fourt, a journeyman baker, on 27 November 1888. Shoemaking had been associated with Stafford since the twelfth century. However, it was not until technologies and methods were developed in the late eighteenth century that a cottage industry became a viable commercial industry. William Horton was the first to link the individual skills of those working in their own homes, first with the opening of the factory in Mill Street. Eventually this resulted in just five shoe manufacturers by 1796, with Horton easily the largest and most successful.

Following a normal day of toil and the evening meal, the two brothers-in-law headed out into the town around eight in the evening. It seems Fourt was soon the worse for drink, although they were still on good terms when seen at a pub in Cherry Street two hours later by Herbert Halden. He later gave evidence in court confirming that Fourt had consumed 'two-pennorth of whisky' and Faulkner 'two-pennorth of port'.

Herbert accompanied the two men home, and in court he said that the cool evening air had accentuated their drunkenness. Hence it was he who helped to see them to the end of County Road, where they lived. On the way, Fourt, who was the worse for drink, fell flat on his face but blamed his brother-

County Road today.

in-law for his fall. Halden helped him all the way to his road, saying the fall, which had scraped a piece of skin from his face, would create a bad first impression on Monday when Fourt started a new job at Mr Noden's premises. Herbert Halden managed to keep the peace until they reached County Road, but things soon deteriorated thereafter.

No sooner had they entered No. 16 than the quarrel resumed. Fourt continued to accuse Faulkner of pushing him, causing him to fall. Mrs Fourt supported her husband and Faulkner ended up ordering both of them out of his house. It was around this point that Faulkner appears to have picked up a knife, one of those he needed for his

The scene of the crime.

work as a shoemaker. This was one of a number of knives kept at their home, kept sharp but unsheathed, and always away from their children. During the minor struggle that followed, this knife caused a minor wound to Mrs Fourt's arm.

Leaving her husband inside, Mrs Fourt ran outside and screamed for help. When she returned she found Faulkner, with the knife still in his hand, leaning over her husband, who was on the floor. Mrs Faulkner took the knife from her husband, cutting her own finger in the process, and imploring, 'Don't do it, for the sake of the children!'

Mrs Fourt noticed blood on her husband's face and got a wet towel to clean him up, believing this to be the result of a bloody nose. However, when she tilted his head back to clean him blood spurted from a gash to his neck. Faulkner, having seen the severity of the wound, sobered up quickly and went for the doctor.

Perhaps Faulkner was still somewhat under the influence when he arrived, for he told the doctor, Charles Reid, that the wound was caused accidentally by the victim pulling the knife back to his own throat. This was later dispelled in court: a medical expert revealed that the victim's exposed throat had been slashed as he jerked his head back to avoid the knife.

By this time the noise had brought Elijah Mottram, Harry Baker, Samuel Morgan and George Arnold from neighbouring houses to see what was going on. Together with Faulkner, and at the request of the doctor, they carried Fourt to the infirmary. By the time they arrived and sought medical help, Fourt was almost dead from loss of blood and

And at the end of County Road today, the present-day gaol.

only lived for a short time. On arrival at the infirmary Faulkner told Mottram he had injured his brother-in-law 'in a passion' but retracted this in his later official statement. The police were sent for and a statement taken from all those present. Faulkner was arrested later that morning.

When news of the crime appeared in the press, Warwickshire police were very interested. It seems the deceased was being sought following the issue of a warrant for his arrest in March 1887. A charge of desertion of a wife and two children had been levelled at him, of a family he had lived with at Henley-in-Arden and Oversley.

As a result of the court case the first Mrs Fourt came to Stafford and identified his body. She even attended the funeral the following Wednesday. A surprising number appeared at the funeral, including the second wife and her father, Mr Spraggins. The press reports the following week were keen to point out the large number present at the funeral, taking great pains to emphasise the majority were women.

Faulkner was found guilty of murder and sentenced to life imprisonment.

AD 1940

AIR RAIDS

WHEN THE PRIME Minister made the now famous speech on the radio in early September 1939, nobody in Britain believed the war would last beyond Christmas that year. (Radio broadcasts were a major source of information and, more importantly, entertainment at the time. Among the most popular programmes were the comedies, which included Tommy Handley in *It's That Man Again* – always abbreviated to *ITMA* – and a certain Rob Wilton, whose recitals always began with 'The day war broke out ...'.)

As the New Year came, with no evidence of a cessation in hostilities, still most of Stafford had seen little of the conflict. At this time it could well have seemed as if the war was someone else's problem.

But there were also those who recognised the very real danger of Stafford being a target for enemy bombers. It was unlikely the town would be a primary target. Yet the danger of enemy bombers dropping their loads here was not to be dismissed. Arriving from German airfields, those aircraft heading for the cities of Liverpool and Manchester would

take advantage of any opportunity to affect as much damage as possible.

Stafford's position on a main railway artery made it an excellent target. The railways themselves could be followed for, sooner or later, all lines led to a sizable town or city. Alternatively, the lines themselves could be severed since transport links are obvious targets. Major centres of population also tend to grow around rivers as a reliable source of water is clearly important, especially when those rivers are navigable. Unlike railway tracks, rivers are very easy to see from the air: they reflect the light, making them easy to see. Follow them, and eventually a potential target will come into view. (Note that Stafford stands on or near the rivers Sow and Trent, as well as on a main railway line.)

Retrospectively, it was inevitable that the town would eventually see a bomb or two. Exactly a year to the day of the declaration of war, an aircraft passed over the area taking a great number of photographs. We know that aircraft was a Junkers Ju88 A-1, for the images survived the war and are now in storage at Keele. Whether these resulted in the second conflict between Stafford and the

A Junkers Ju88 A-1 dropping bombs over Britain.

Axis Powers is uncertain. Yet just thirty-six days later the air-raid sirens warned residents to head for cover.

Initially the townsfolk thought it yet another drill. Looking up they saw what they perceived as 'one of ours', which increased reaction time substantially – until anti-aircraft fire was aimed at the plane from the roof of the Universal Grinding factory building. This aircraft was untouched and flew on to its target, but a second bomber soon followed behind. When a teacher ventured out of the air-raid shelter, seeking information which would reassure her girls, she could not have imagined what she actually saw. The bomber dropped its load and these bombs exploded just a few hundred yards away.

Next day the German propaganda machine reported how this lone bomber, having targeted Stafford, had begun its low-level bombing run with the main factories and outbuildings within sight. The radio broadcast went on to state that these buildings had been literally blown into the air by the force of the explosions. The *Stafford Chronicle*'s version was a little different (a situation reflected up and down the country, usually for reasons relating to morale).

As reported by the local press, there were just four bombs dropped. However, one failed to go off on impact and the bomb squad were sent for. These experts moved the bomb into a crater created by one of the other weapons, where it was detonated under controlled conditions. Damage was restricted to broken windows. Two girls were injured by shards of glass, one hospitalised and the second deemed fit enough to be sent home to recover. Just eleven houses suffered damage to glass, while a couple of panes at the public baths were dislodged. The German aircraft was chased off by two British fighters. Its fate is unknown.

In the town centre shoppers had carried on with their daily lives, only running for cover when the explosions were heard. On the roads traffic was already heavy and moving only slowly. With their only other option being to abandon their vehicles and run for cover, the motorists opted to remain at the wheel and continue on their journey, albeit slowly. The incident brought home the very real dangers of war and local officials feared this was only the start. As a result, the following month saw a large storehouse dedicated to storing the hundreds of shrouds bought in especially for the anticipated casualties.

Overall, however, Stafford was considered a 'safe town' and in June 1940 some 1,600 children arrived by

Spitfire MK XVi. (Chowells, CC-BY-SA-25)

train from Ramsgate in Kent. Ramsgate's coastal location made it a dangerous place to be and evacuees on station platforms were a common sight. They still needed to be educated and a shift system was employed whereby local children sat at the desks during one part of the day and evacuees for the remainder.

Christmas pantomimes continued, the children putting on their version of *Sleeping Beauty*. Years later one girl, who had landed the title role, admitted that while in the sleep which lasted 100 years she had opened one eye to see what was going on. Her attention was focused on one of the 'older boys', who had

tears streaming down his face – not an emotional reaction to a sad tale but an ordinary boy feeling terribly homesick.

Examining the Air-Raid Patrol Warden's records for the entire war shows how the warning sirens were sounded just 284 times for real air raids, not drills. By far the busiest period was these last four months of 1940, a period sometimes referred to as the Midlands Blitz. Yet this 'busy' period hardly affected Stafford, which saw a maximum of just three further raids during the whole war.

On 22 October an incendiary device fell in a field close to the town. Damage was so minimal that one member of the Home Guard managed to bring it under control on his own. Records of the other two raids are sketchy, both identified solely by the spent bullet cases fired by anti-aircraft guns around the end of the year of 1940.

To help the war, Stafford raised the money to purchase their own Spitfire, which they named the *Staffordian*.

BIBLIOGRAPHY

The Staffordshire Advertiser, various

Butters, Paul, *Stafford: The Story of a Thousand Years*, Crescent Publishing Co., 1979

Cherry, J.L., *Stafford in Olden Times*, J. & C. Mort, 1890

Payne, W., *Stafford Gaol and its Associations*, J. Hitchings, printer and publisher, 1887

Powner, Jonathon R., *A Duty Done: A History of Fire-Fighting in Staffordshire*, Staffordshire County Council, 1987

Wilkins, Dudley, *Fragments of Stafford's Past*, R.W. Hourd & Son, 1932

If you enjoyed this book, you may also be interested in…

IMAGES OF ENGLAND

AROUND
STAFFORD

ROY LEWIS

Around Stafford
ROY LEWIS

This book reproduces more than 200 fascinating photographs of Stafford and the surrounding area including the villages of Gnosall, Haughton and Sandon, revealing the sweeping changes that have taken place in local streets, buildings, schools, churches and factories. It remembers many local events, from pageants, sports meetings and royal visits to many other special occasions. With pictures from the County Museum at Shugborough and from private collections, it will delight residents and visitors alike.

978 0 7524 1811 7

Haunted Staffordshire
PHILIP SOLOMON

With heart-stopping accounts of apparitions, manifestations and related supernatural phenomena, this collection of stories contains both new and well-known spooky stories from around Staffordshire. Compiled by the *Wolverhampton Express & Star*'s own psychic agony uncle Philip Solomon, this terrifying assortment of tales includes details of long-reported poltergeist activity at Sinai House, strange goings-on at the Gladstone Pottery Museum and even a reported visitation from author J.R.R. Tolkien in Leek! It is sure to fascinate everyone with an interest in the area's haunted history.

978 0 7524 6168 7

Visit our website and discover thousands of other History Press books.

www.thehistorypress.co.uk

Lightning Source UK Ltd.
Milton Keynes UK
UKOW03f1343250713

214347UK00004B/76/P